LUCINDA LAMBTON'S
A to Z of BRITAIN

By the same author

VANISHING VICTORIANA

TEMPLES OF CONVENIENCE

CHAMBERS OF DELIGHT

BEASTLY BUILDINGS

AN ALBUM OF CURIOUS HOUSES

MAGNIFICENT MENAGERIE

TEMPLES OF CONVENIENCE/CHAMBERS OF DELIGHT
(REVD EDITION)

LUCINDA LAMBTON'S
A *to* Z *of* BRITAIN

HarperCollins*Publishers*

HarperCollins*Publishers*
77–85 Fulham Palace Road,
Hammersmith, London w6 8jb

Published by
HarperCollins*Publishers* 1996
3 5 7 9 8 6 4 2

A catalogue record for this book is
available from the British Library

ISBN 0 00 255694 4

Endpapers from G. F. Watts's
memorial tiles (see Glazed Glories).
Chapter opening initials from The
South Kensington Alphabet
designed by Godfrey Sykes (see
Glazed Glories)
Jacket illustration by
Tom Errington

Set in Caslon 540

Printed in Great Britain by
The Bath Press, Bath

ACKNOWLEDGEMENTS

Dedicated with love and thanks to Neil Crombie, Andrew Gosling, Christine Hall and Jamie Muir for their masterly direction of the films *The Alphabet of Britain* on BBC2 and to Franny Moyle for *Y Oh Why?*.

I would especially like to thank Will Wyatt for his trust and enthusiasm, Alan Yentob, Paul Hayman and Michael Jackson must be thanked for giving the green light to so many of the films as well as Duncan Dallas and Eddie Mirzoff for the excellence of their over-seeing. Michael Oakes must be praised for his delightful drawings, David Oliver for his gothic calligraphy as well as Matt Fowler for his ever reliable photography. Rebecca Lloyd has been the perfect sympathetic editor. Philip Lewis has shown unending patience along with Linde Hardaker and I must thank Sonia Dobie for the design of the jacket. Three cheers for Michael Fishwick for bringing the book into being. Justine Fulford and Deborah Parrish have shown unstinting assistance and valuable help and my sweetheart husband Perry has been unswerving in his affection, advice and support.

Heartfelt thanks are also due to the following few!

Her Majesty the Queen (The Royal Dairy, Windsor); Mohammed Al Fayed; Aldershot Military Museum; Father Andrew; Cathie Arrington; Paul Atlas; Revd W. Awdry; Nigel Babbage; Sophie Badham; Marta Baker; L.H. Barker; Sue Barnes; Francesca Barron; Victor Bartlett; M. Bergin; Val Berk; Mary Beverage; Mark Bills; Mrs Bint; Peter and Chrissie Blake; Wilfred Blunt; Tony Bolton; John Bond; Revd Colin Boswell; Colin Bowden; Nedgeley Boyd-Harte; Mrs Brennan; British Cement Association; Jayne Britton; Beatty Bronson; Alistair Brown; R.J. Brown; Lynne and Richard Bryant; David Bryn; Brynteg Comprehensive School; Kevin Bryson; Sam Bull; David Burkett; Lady Jennifer Bute; the late Marquis of Bute; Christine Buttner; Ailsa Campbell; Luke Cardiff; Roy Challiner; Dr Gordon Chancellor; Darrell Charlton; Brian Chilvers; Thomas Chitty; Ian Churchill; Liz Clare; Martin Clarke; Paula Cliffe; Martyn Clift; Dr John F. Cole; Michael Cole; Howard Colvin; Basil Comely; Brian Compton; Mr and Mrs A.A. Cooper; Mr Cork; R. Cork; Dan Cruikshank; Tracy Cullen; Father Curran; Father Cuthbert; Geoff Cutting; Mr Dalrymple; Dr Richard Danckwerts; the late Mrs Davies; Warren Davies; Hermine Demoriane; Pauline Dickson; Major General R. Dixon; Dick Dodd; Lindsay Dodd; Richard Downing; Beverley Doyle; Mr Draper; Johnny Dumfries; Nick Dummer; Martin Durrant; Miss Grace Dyson; Marie Edwards; Sue Ellison; Elaine M. English; Tom Errington; Trevor Evans; Valentine Evans; Richard Farrington; Mrs Fellingham; Angela Fox; Sue Freathy; Anne Froggett; Liz Gammon; Sean Garner; Eleanor Gawne; David George; Christopher Gibbs; Mr and Mrs Gilbert; Mr Goodard; Ian Gow; Francis Graham; Nick Green; Miss Greville; Andrew Griffin; David Griffin; David J. Griffin; Norman Grigg; Revd Val Hamer; Nadene Hansen; Alex Hanson; Lady Rose Hare; Revd Harkness; David Harris; David Harrison; Huckleberry Harrod; Wilhelmine Harrod; Revd John Harvey; John Haslam; Steve Hayward; Gwyn Headley; Myles Hildyard; Marion

Hill; Richard Hill; M.J. Hill; Min Hogg; Robert Holden; Bob Holmes; Revd Ben Hopkinson; David Horne; Hounslow Library; Martin Howe; Dr Huggins; John Humpage; Nick Humphrey; Revd Jeremy Hurst; Chris Hutchinson; Revd Patrick Hutton; Norman and Valerie Illingworth; Andrew Jackson; Jean and Frank Jackson; Jan Asprey ; Patrick Janssens; Jeff Whiteman ; Richard Jeffrey; R.H. Jeffries; Mr Jennings; Lucy Johnson; Caroline Jones; Penny Jones; Supt. Jones; Stuart Kassimir; Michael Kearney; Kederminster Library; Kelly's Funeral Directors; Muriel Kemp; Angela King; Kinloch; Tim Knox; La Reunion des Musees Nationaux (Versailles); Ian Lane; Mr Larkworthy; Dr Paul Larmour; Linen Hall Library, Belfast; Andy Lockyer; London Library; D. Lopez; Mr Lowe; Lt Col Frank Tredget; Rachel Lynch; William Macbean; Richard MacCormack; Aled Madoc; Dr W.A. Maguire; Patrick Maher; Ian Maine; John Martin; Mary Evans Picture Library; Hanne H. Mason; Lona Mason; Miss Betty Matthews; Gayle Mault; Maggie Mawhinny; Gordon Maxwell; Mr Maxwell; Mr and Mrs Ian MacArthur; Jim McGeary; James McStrabick; Father Michael; Mr and Mrs Lawrence Miller; Terry Mitchell; David Moore; Jan Morgan; Martin Morgan; Tom Morgan; Dr Richard Mortimer; Colonel Morton; Richard Morton; the late Major Malcolm Munthe; Peggy Murphy; Enid Musson; Grant Muter; Andrew Norris; Eddie Norton; Dr Andrew J. Norton; Steve O'Brien; Helen O'Neill; Jerome Oliver; John Outram; Tim Owen; Gill Page; John Paine; Francesca Paolozzi; John Parkinson; Ernie Patterson; Willie Payne; Martin Pearce; Steve Peet; Revd David Pemberton; David Perman; Nigel Philpott; Richard Pickett; the late Mr Pike; Elaine Pilbeam; Jonathan Pilkington; Rebecca Pinto; Victoria Pirie; Colin Price; Paul Pritchard; Mr and Mrs Arthur Quarmby; Keith Quirke; Sean Rafferty; Revd Paul M. Reece; Reflections (especially Diane); Angela Reid; Margaret Richardson; Mike Riley; Wayne Roberts; Annie Robertson; David Rowbotham; Royal Alexandra and Albert School; Royal Holloway College; Jason Russell; Michael and Elizabeth Sandford; Sandra Royal; Vivienne Schuster; Bill Scott of the River House Hotel, Skipool Creek, Blackpool; Mr M. Shafiq; Dave Sheard; Paul Shephard–Watson; Malcolm R. Shifrin; John Sibun; Isobel Sinden; Elizabeth and Angus Smith; Lady Soames; Julian Spicer; Peter Stebbings; Revd Tom Steele; Wilma Stewart; Brenda Stone; John Strangward; Colin Stuart; Neil Sumner; Philip Swindells; Charles Tate; Graham Teasdill; Mrs Templeton; Phramaha Term; Charles and Jessica Thomas; Tamsin Thomas; Geoffrey Thompson; Mrs Doris Thompson; Bob Thomson and Son; Jane Thorn; Julia Thornton; Peter Thornton; Eric Throssell; Revd R.D. Tomkinson; John Turnbull; Dave Turton; Ulster Folk and Transport Museum; United Grand Lodge of England; University College Hospital and the Archive Department; Alan Unwin; Carole Vincent; Mr and Mrs Walker; Mr Walsh; Katherine Ward; Janet Watson; Linsey Watson; Mr and Mrs Welby; Philip Wellstead White; Geoff West; Julie Westney; Revd Wheeler; David White; Mr and the late Mrs Whitehead; Jeff Whiteman; Bill Wild; Mr Wildgust; Keith Williams; Mrs Williams; Mrs L.D. Williamson; Anna Wood; Henrietta Wood; T. Wylie; Rhona Young.

CONTENTS

ART NOUVEAU 1

BELFAST 6

CONCRETE 13

DORSET'S DELIGHT 18

EASTERN 23

FUN DAYS OUT 32

GLAZED GLORIES 38

HEATHROW 43

ISLE OF BUTE 49

SIR JOHN'S MUSEUM 53

KENSAL GREEN 61

LOVED ONES 71

M25 77

NOTTINGHAM'S PRIDE 86

OPULENT ENDINGS 90

PRISONERS OF WAR 96

QUIET EVENINGS IN 102

RHUM 108

SOUTHSIDE 113

TEMPLES 117

UNDER THE GROUND 122

VICARS 127

WAX 134

XANADU 140

Y OH WHY ? 144

ZETA 149

SELECT BIBLIOGRAPHY 152

INDEX 154

ART NOUVEAU

THE sinuous architectural forms which were to become known as 'Art Nouveau' writhed their way through Europe during the turn of the last century, but their tendrils barely touched England's shores. (They flourished, of course, in Scotland, although even Charles Rennie Mackintosh was careful to untangle their twists and turns.) For the English architectural profession, however, it was the Arts and Crafts movement that reigned supreme. Because that movement loathed sham and loved honesty, the fashion for 'the Squirm' – as they called Art Nouveau – was denounced. It was sneeringly said that such an outlandish style obscured the construction with its 'fidgety, vulgar obtrusiveness quite destructive of all dignity and repose'. Even Alfred Gilbert – the master sculptor of curvilinear forms – had weighed in, denouncing Art Nouveau architecture as belonging to the 'duffers' paradise'.

There were colourful counterblasts, with the architect Charles Harrison Townsend retorting that the Arts and Crafts movement's cry for simplicity was 'due to omission, a negation that is a poor substitute for invention, a cowardice pretending to be courage'. He himself had grasped the nettle boldly when designing the Whitechapel Art Gallery and the Horniman Museum in London as well as St Mary's

Church at Great Warley in Essex; all of them related in style to their Art Nouveau counterparts abroad.

The style is rare in England and is therefore all the more exhilarating when you come upon it. One such find is to be made in Hope Street in Liverpool, when wham! you are whacked in the face by the sight of the twirling gates of the Philharmonic Public House. They were designed by H. Blomfield Bare, who went the whole hog with the Art Nouveau style in Liverpool, every bit as much as did Horta in Brussels and Hector Guimard with his famed Métro entrances in Paris. The Philharmonic Hotel, as it was originally called, was built between 1898 and 1900 with a lush interior decorated by artists from the University School of Art, under the overall direction of Walter Thomas. Mr Blomfield Bare blazed away with a series of repoussé copper panels of various creatures, while Charles Allen was responsible for beautifully bosomed caryatids – all modelled from a friend of his called Mrs Ryan. This is a gin palace that gleams. Its superbly sleek finish owes much to having been fashioned by ships' carpenters and craftsmen who, temporarily laid off from the luxurious interiors of the great liners, were ready to create such splendours on shore.

In Windsor, Art Nouveau iron writhes away once again but this time decorating a royal tomb rather than a tempting saloon. It is the memorial by Alfred

Gilbert to the Duke of Clarence in the Albert Memorial Chapel within the walls of Windsor Castle. Queen Victoria's grandson, Prince Albert Victor, Duke of Clarence, had died aged twenty-eight in January 1892 and within a week Gilbert was commissioned to commemorate his short life. The memorial was to take him thirty-six tormented years to finish – and was largely the cause of his bankruptcy. The work was not even completed on the deaths of Edward VII and Queen Alexandra, who had asked him to do it in the first place. So perilous was his penury that he was reduced to selling casts of the tomb before it was finished to make ends meet. For this he was never forgiven by the King.

The Albert Chapel had been restored for Queen Victoria in 1869 – set a-shimmering by George Gilbert Scott and with marble and mosaics by Triqueti – and Alfred Gilbert was to beat this flamboyance at its own game. The young Duke, heir to the throne, who according to James Pope-Hennessy was 'as heedless and aimless as a gleaming goldfish in a crystal bowl', lies with white marble face and hands in the bronze and brass uniform of the 10th Hussars. Saintly 'guardians' stand over all, above angels whose wings and robes follow the flow. St George, in crustacean-like aluminium armour, languorously shows off the shapely grace of Art Nouveau. Then there is St Michael – embraced by his own wings and those on his helmet – standing giant-like with a miniature city at his feet. St Elizabeth releases cascades of scarlet roses from beneath her cloak and the silver- and gold-robed Virgin is entwined with the golden stems of a purple rose. This grille around the royal sarcophagus is a miraculous manifestation of the architectural style that Gilbert professed to loathe. His work, though, must be thought of in terms of giant jewels rather than of architecture in miniature.

Eros – scarcely appreciated today as a great monument in the Art Nouveau style – was Gilbert's first important commission. It was designed to commemorate the life of the philanthropist Anthony Ashley Cooper, 7th Earl of Shaftesbury. With the God of Love and with fountains of green copper waves filled with merbabies and fish portraying Lord Shaftesbury's overflowing goodness, this was one of the first symbolic public monuments in the country. Not being of 'the suit and trouser brigade' it caused a sensation and was greeted with hoots of both delight and derision. 'A dripping sickening mess', with 'Cupid' firing his arrows into the midst of parading prostitutes, it was thought to be a wildly unsuitable memorial to the great Earl. The monument heralded Gilbert's financial downfall, costing him over twice as much as he was paid for it. Years later, when he was in the quagmire of poverty, debt and unfinished work, his supporters unwisely appealed to George Bernard Shaw. His reply was pleasant: that the 'dishonest sculptor should be shot … [but] for Gilbert, shooting is too honourable a death. He should be drowned in the fountain with which he has disfigured Piccadilly.' However, George Frampton the sculptor wrote to Ellen Terry that Piccadilly should be 'destroyed and rebuilt merely as a setting for Gilbert's jewel'!

The monument to Queen Alexandra in Marlborough Gate in London was Gilbert's last huzzah. Love is enthroned, supported by Faith and Hope, directing a child across the River of Life. It was unveiled on 8 June 1930, with a dedication by the Archbishop of Canterbury, and with choirs singing an Elgar motet to the words of John Masefield.

In Europe the Art Nouveau style was thought to give streets an elegant countenance, enticing you with its charms into each café and shop. In England such 'charmingly cheap and commercial ploys' – as the critics contemptuously called them – were barely put to the test. Kodak was an exception with a fancy

'Love directing a child across the river of life' – Gilbert's monument to Queen Alexandra

shop façade in the Strand and a photograph survives of another's ornate interior in the Brompton Road. Harrods applied the style to the meat hall, with a series of ceramic scenes of hunting and herding designed by W.J. Neatby in 1901. He was head of the architectural department at Doulton's and was one of the few designers in Britain to apply brilliant colour to Art Nouveau designs. The Edward Everard Building in Bristol was his particular triumph. It was built in 1900 as a printing house and its ceramic façade is a shining show-case of the trade. Everard printed an exquisite book telling the tale of this architectural decoration that 'has called forth an enthusiasm which partakes of the nature of disturbed sensations'. He saw the building as a 'trophy' to the Middle Ages, 'when the atmosphere was warm with the homeliness of pure and thoughtful craft'. A life-sized ceramic figure of Gutenberg – the father of

'A trophy to the Middle Ages' in Bristol

printing – works at his press, surrounded by his 1490s alphabet. Facing him is William Morris who revived the craft, surrounded by his 1890s alphabet. The spirit of literature touches the tips of both presses with her wings and the allegorical figure of truth, with a mirror and lamp, presides. Such was the 'unusual interest' at the building's unveiling that the police were called to control the wondering crowds.

At Compton, near Guildford, there is a chapel that whirls into a web of Art Nouveau decoration. It was designed, built and decorated by a woman who had never built anything before in her life and was never to do so again. She was Mary Watts, wife of G.F. Watts the great Victorian painter and although he paid for it – painting a picture especially to finance the work – he played no part in the chapel's construction. It was built by amateurs, except for a blacksmith, a local builder and an architect called Redmayne, who supervised Mrs Watts supervising the labour force. Within three years the chapel was built – a gleaming brick beacon, which Mrs Watts had hoped would blend into the countryside. It most certainly does not, never will and is all the more glorious because of that. A Greek cross in vivid terracotta, the building has a ground plan of a circle run through with a cross symbolizing Eternity and Faith. Every inch of its intricate Celtic and Art Nouveau decoration has a message from Mrs Watts. The exterior, with friezes of the spirits of Love, Hope, Truth and Light, has the Tree of Life climbing each buttress. The doorway is surrounded by a choir of angels – their wings entwined with Celtic cord, pierced through with peacock's eyes. Inside you are enfolded by the glow of rich and dark colours and by endlessly interweaving lines, woven, according to Mrs Watts, 'as it were into a mystical garment'. The roots of the Tree of Life writhe beneath the sombrely beautiful 'winged messengers' – great feathered giantesses 'presenting the light and the dark side of things'. Those of the light have haunting faces gazing out and those of the dark, their backs turned: 'Night and Day, Growth and Decay. Ebb and Flow and Joy and Sorrow.' They stand two by two around the walls all grasping the sharply raised 'Celtic Nouveau' cord containing symbolic cameos. It is all made of gesso – fibre soaked in plaster of Paris – fashioned into panels at Limmerslease, their house nearby, which had been built with the error of forgetting a staircase from the first to the second floor! The panels were then attached to a metal framework on the chapel walls and further enriched to reach their final splendour. A gilded message which reads: 'But the Souls of the

Righteous are in the Hands of God', supports the thick vaulted ribs – covered with cherubs – that soar up, past crimson-clad seraphs to meet 'The Circle of the Eternal'.

Despite living only half a mile away, Watts saw his wife's *tour de force* only once – and then by chance – when he followed her out on a walk. She wrote, 'He had not before realised what I had aspired to in the matter of this glorified wallpaper, and spoke with his usual generous appreciation.'

Thanks to Mary Watts and precious few others we can thrill to the riotous lines of the Art Nouveau style in England.

Mary Watts creating her 'winged messengers'

BELFAST

FROM the moment you breathe in the air of Belfast your senses are stoked up with the rich spirit of the place; with the uncommon charm and cheerfulness of the people – ever heartening and helpful – along with the beauty of so many of its buildings. All this in a city that has few parallels in switchback-like changes of fortune.

Once the linen capital of the world, Belfast went on to harbour the world's greatest shipyard as well as its largest rope works and tobacco factory and these periods of prosperity are reflected, gem-like, in the city's architecture. Buildings from the late 1700s onwards proclaim the prosperity of 'Linenapolis' while Victorian and Edwardian palaces of commerce still holler triumphantly at one another in the very centre of the city, across Donegall Square and the City Hall – a symbol of civic pride that has few rivals under the sun.

It was the first Marquess of Donegal who was largely responsible for laying the elegant architectural and prosperous financial foundations of eighteenth-century Belfast. He built many of the first public buildings as well as churches and he gave the lands for the Poor House of 1774 as well as for the White Linen Hall of 1783 – both of them vastly important to the development of the city. The Poor House 'for the employment of idle beggars… and for the reception of old and diseased poor' had taken three years to build, with money raised by such ventures as George A. Stevens's 'Lecture on Heads' which produced £1 2s 7d! Children were later admitted and it was thanks to them being 'employed' with spinning wheels that Belfast's first cotton mill was born. With its success there followed the full-scale mass production of both cotton and linen and, with that, a booming and blooming Belfast.

The White Linen Hall – where linen was bought and sold – was the symbolic centre of the new linen lord's empire. It was built where the City Hall stands today. Building after building proclaimed the new affluence of the city, with such architectural delicacies as the First Presbyterian Church by Roger Mulholland setting standards in the late 1700s. In 1844 Thomas Jackson designed a feast of sugary stucco to drop in great pendants from the ceiling of St Malachy's Roman Catholic Church in Alfred Street. Queen Victoria gave Belfast a city charter in 1888. She and Albert had been to Belfast in 1849 and Sir Charles Brett, in his book *The Buildings of Belfast*, tells us of a pearl of a poem that was written at the time:

> *She came in the grace of her*
> *womanly love,*
> *An Irishman's ardent*

affection to move;
Her 'Cushia machree'
Filled her heart with such glee,
That oft to her Albert, she
said with delight –
'His head may be wrong, but
his heart's in the right'.
Hurrah for the Queen! may
posterity see
Each year on this island a
grand jubilee:
May Minstrels arise
To contend for the prize;
And bards, yet unborn, sing
the joys of the past –
Of VICTORIA, and ALBERT,
and loyal Belfast.

A rich representation of the Queen was carved in Durham Street. After the building was demolished, she was rescued by the National Trust and now stands in a stable yard – clad in frills and festoons of stone lace – waiting for a new home.

There are pleasing architectural details throughout the entire city with some thousands of faces and creatures peering down on to the streets. At McCausland's warehouse in Victoria Street five vast heads representing the five continents loom over the fruits of their lands. Africa has a grim chain writhing through its pomegranates.

More than anyone it was Sir Charles Lanyon who built Belfast, establishing the rip-roaringly eclectic variety of styles that can still be seen surging through the city today. With his heavy-as-lead Crumlin Road gaol of 1845 and his light-as-feather Queen's University of 1849, Lanyon's horizons were broad. He became Mayor of Belfast in 1862 and Member of Parliament in 1866.

The Gothic glories of St Malachy's

His Palm House in the Botanic Gardens is one of the earliest curvilinear glass houses to have been built and the oldest still standing today. The foundation stone was laid in 1839, nine years before the Great Palm House at Kew, Richard Turner of Dublin being the builder of both. Flying from Belfast to Heathrow you can spot the three glass palaces – two at Kew and one at Syon – all together within the plastic frame of the airplane window. But Ulster's Palm House can boast of just as much beauty. The bulbous dome was designed in 1862.

The Botanic Gardens has even more exotic charms within its Tropical Ravine, the only one made by man in the world. It was created in 1886 by Charles McKim, the curator of the gardens, a man of whom it was said that his fingers were so green that he could raise a prize bloom from a seed planted in an empty flower pot. Stepping into the ravine's redbrick

'Ganging up' in the 1940s beside the 1840s Botanic Garden Palm House

building is like finding yourself in a fanciful fairytale. Suddenly steeped in boiling climes, the air heavy with humidity, you are surrounded on all sides by trees and plants of banana and cinnamon, coffee, sugar cane, aloe, ivory nut, rubber, bamboo, guava and grapefruit. There is a small chain hanging amidst the leaves which, with one tug, activates a waterfall to roar through the palms, the mosses and the great ferns. I found a lively link with the gardens in that my great-grandfather exhibited a twenty-two pound bunch of black grapes there, at the Great International Fruit and Flower Show of 1874.

Belfast is particularly ennobled by its surroundings, with the mountainous crags of Cave Hill framed by the grand old buildings of the city centre. Stand beneath the green domes of the City Hall and you see the full majesty of nature flanked by the Linen Hall Library – a more delightfully dignified institution of the old school would be hard to find – while on the other side of the street the towers of the vast Scottish Providential Society rear into the sky. Cave Hill, with a silhouette of a colossal human countenance, has all the appearance of a sleeping Napoleon and is known locally as 'Napoleon's Nose'. I am indebted to Jonathan Bardon in his excellent book *Belfast* for this poem by Alice Milligan:

> *Look up from the street of the city,*
> *Look high beyond towers and mast,*
> *What hand of what Titan sculptor*
> *Smote the crags on the mountain vast?*
> *Made when the world was fashioned,*
> *Meant with the world to last,*
> *The glorious face of a sleeper*
> *That slumbers above Belfast.*

The northernmost mountain of a range that marches up to the west of Belfast, Cave Hill was once the centre of festivities for Easter Monday celebrations. Throughout the seventeenth, eigteenth and early nineteenth centuries, it was to its peak as 'the rising sun gilded the waves', that the whole of the town trooped. The poet William Reed wrote of the revels in 1818:

> *… Now group on group is seen to follow far*
> *Like a rabble army in array –*
> *On foot, on horse, coach, jingle cart and car,*
> *Towards the Hill of Caves they wend their way…*
> *Here you might mark life's anxious, ardent*
> *   strugglers*
> *Of every hue – whate'er their cast or calling –*
> *Musicians, pedlars, show-men, dupes and jugglers –*
> *No Babel tower had echoed to such bawling!*
> *Carousing, begging, singing, laughing, brawling,*
> *The fiddle's flourish, and the bag-pipe's*
> *grunting…*

Drinking and dancing 'with a graceful knee' they pranced 'Caledonia's reels' as they quaffed 'the cup of glee'.

There are few places where you can quaff in such superb splendour as in the Crown Liquor Saloon in Great Victoria Street and, if there was ever a symbol of the beauty and bravery of the place, this is it. Time and time again this public house has suffered from IRA bomb damage – it stands opposite the Europa Hotel – and time and again it has risen glittering afresh from the ashes. With its extraordinarily rich decoration from 1885 this little building is a brilliant beacon of Belfast that burns bright in the hearts of all who have seen it. Etched mirrors painted in vivid hues rise up from behind the sweep of the marble-covered ceramic bar. With richly carved wooden

screens, gilded Corinthian columns and a wealth of pattern under your feet and over your head, you are encased with ornamental splendour. Heraldic creatures bearing such mottoes as 'Fortune Favours the Brave' and 'Love your Country' guard entrances to entrancing 'snugs' into which customers can plunge for picturesque privacy.

When William Ritchie came to town in 1791 and built the first shipyard, he began what was to develop into one of Belfast's greatest commercial coups.

> *Ingenious Ritchie! Commerce now may smile*
> *And shed her blessings o'er Hibernia's Isle.*
> *Go, teach her sons to raise the ships on high*
> *The pointed mast high towering in the sky.*

So wrote Thomas Romney Robinson in 'The Triumph of Commerce' when he was only nine years old. In 1859 Edward James Harland went into partnership with Gustav Wolff and the world's largest shipyard was born. It was to build ships of outstanding efficiency and splendour: such giantesses as the *Oceanic* whose first-class dining saloon was decked out with a glass dome and pillars, murals and mottoes.

'Bicycling away their lives' in the Titanic *gym*

Or the *Olympic*, whose splendid saloon can still, most surprisingly, be sat in at the White Swan Hotel at Alnwick in Northumberland, whither it was taken when the liner was dismantled in the 1930s.

Her sister ship the *Titanic* is, of course, a mournful memory especially to the people of Belfast, many of whom are descended from the workforce who built the great liner. They have their daily reminder of the disaster, too, with the hauntingly beautiful memorial by Charles Brock that stands in the city centre.

The sea was smooth as glass when the *Titanic* struck an iceberg. After the miserably inadequate number of lifeboats had been filled – some disgrace-fully not so – all the remaining 1517 passengers simply had to await their fate for another two hours with some stalwartly bicycling away their lives in the gym. From the safe-haven horror of the lifeboats, the great ship, ablaze with light in the night, was seen almost to stand on her head. There was a whooshing crash as all the furniture, including five grand pianos, shot forward, while the wretched passengers on deck slipped and slid into their icy graves. All this to the strains of the valiant string ensemble playing away at the Episcopal hymn 'Autumn'.

Sinclair Seamen's Presbyterian Church in Corporation Square (again by our old friend Lanyon) was like a holy harbour of refuge to the thousands of seamen who poured through Belfast. It was founded in 1832 'for the promotion of the religious improvement of the Belfast seamen' and it was transformed into a sparkling seafarers' paradise in the early 1900s. The Revd Samuel Cochrain was responsible, a man of whom it was said 'in his amiable and optimistic flight, he never allowed his wings to droop'. Nor indeed did he. When designing his church he soared to heights of adventurous originality unmatched in any other church in the British Isles. The pulpit with its great sweep of handsomely carved wood was his first port of call in 1903, the prow of the ship *Mizpah* being added thirty years later. A green starboard light as well as a red port and white mainsail lights all came from Guinness barges on the River Liffey in Dublin. The brass wheel and the capstan are from an American ship, sunk off the coast of Scotland during the First World War. Idiosyncratic details abound, such as the miniature lifeboat collection boxes that set sail every service for funds. A linoleum anchor at the altar is for the bride and groom to stand on during the wedding service – 'safely anchored for life' – and a ship's wheel and flags of welcome are embedded into the floor. There are brasses in the shape of bells and anchors, as well as a lighthouse, a rudder and a life belt. I could go on until the fleet comes in… The Sinclair Seamen's Church has been variously described as 'a lighthouse with its beam still warning of the dangers that a Christian may encounter on the Sea of Life' and as 'a mighty rock riding proudly above the waves while the unresting sea of sin beats around'. Sadly it stands today in a sea of roaring traffic.

Belfast is still marching forth with architectural gusto. A colossal round concert hall based on the Philharmonie at Munich is being built – on the banks of the River Lagan – by architects Robinson and McIlwaine, whilst in Bradbury Place the glitzy Manhattan Club is flashing the night away.

Having shown such resilience and courage in times of trouble, what triumphs could lie ahead for the city given times of peace.

A lifeboat collection box

CONCRETE

THESE are stirring times for concrete! After years of despised disgrace – maligned by many as today's most soul-crushing invention – concrete is at long last being relished for its full potential. In fact, there was never any need for it to be monstrous and it is by no means modern: the earliest known concrete – the floor of a hut in Yugoslavia – dates back to 5600 BC.

It has been a long haul from the structural splendours of ancient Rome – which had a surprising number of concrete buildings – to its rebirth today, but architects are once again realizing what splendours could and should lie ahead with this brilliantly versatile material.

Like stepping stones through history, concrete buildings from throughout the ages can be found in Britain. The Norman Abbey at Reading was built of the material *circa* 1130 and Britain's tallest spire at Salisbury Cathedral has safely stood on concrete foundations since the mid-1200s. A giant figure of Neptune was built of the material near Bristol in 1750. Then, of course, there is Old Father Thames, sculpted in concrete for the Great Exhibition of 1851 by Rafaele Monti, who sat at the source of the river in Lechlade in Gloucestershire between 1958–74, and is now nearby at Lechlade Lock.

Concrete was reborn with a boom in the early 1800s, when Joseph Aspdin invented the superior Portland Cement – cement, stone, sand and water being the four ingredients of the rock cake that is concrete. So successful, indeed, was his invention that his son William designed a mansion in 1850 – Portland Hall – built entirely of concrete. Fragments of the house still survive, and are thought to be the earliest commercially produced concrete details in the country. William Aspdin then opened at Gateshead the largest cement works in the world. These were palatial premises, proudly proclaiming the importance of the material, with urns, balustrades, a triumphal arch topped with a twenty-one-foot-high Royal coat of arms; and the giant figure of Hercules overall, struggling in vain to separate bricks bonded with Portland Cement. Aspdin's invention was produced in this palace, then packed into wooden barrels and shipped off down the Tyne. Miraculously – through misfortune – some of those barrel-shaped blocks still survive on the Isle of Sheppey in Kent, where the very walls of a pub are built out of their barrel-moulded forms. In 1848 a consignment of concrete had run aground at nearby Rats Bay and the ship – the *Lucky Escape* – was pillaged by locals who thought that the barrels contained whisky galore! The cement had set hard in the water but was put to excellent and suitable use, building the pub – the Ship on Shore.

When the possibilities of concrete dawned, they were damned every bit as much as they were desired. As early as the 1860s and 1870s controversy raged as to whether or not it should appear naked, in its unadorned state, or be disguised with old and familiar fig leaves. 'Here is a real chance', wrote one critic, 'for doing something new on the basis of a new material and method … all this dressing up of the new … in the old cloak, is labour thrown away in making a sham.' Another saw cleanliness as concrete's greatest advantage, with 'no hollow spaces to harbour vermin'.

In its sheer and unadorned state it was the very antithesis of the architectural exuberance of the Victorian age, yet dolling up the material was deemed a disaster of duplicity. What should and what could it look like anyway? And to confuse the issue further, some 'shams' were superb – notably the details on London's Grosvenor Hotel at Victoria, where faces peer out from flowers and foliage.

In 1883 the architect Frederick Pepys Cockerell triumphantly trod the tightrope between the two factions at Down Hall in Essex, a stylish stately home built of concrete – now a hotel – with decorations that, far from betraying the material, bring it out in glorious relief. Panels of sgraffito work adorn the walls – made of cement that has been incised through to the concrete. They are all the work of a Mr Wormleighton and a Mr Wise. For the rest of the building plain bands of Portland Cement are set into sea-shingle concrete.

Concrete statelies were never to become all the rage, although in Surrey in 1872 a Mr G.B. Edwards invited readers of *The Builder* to come and inspect his 'Handsome Gothic house in the new material Portland cement concrete'. It was open for ten days to anyone 'presenting his card to the gardener on the premises'. Most surprisingly, Osborne House – the great Italianate pile built on the Isle of Wight for Queen Victoria – had a great deal of concrete used in its construction.

While such buildings attempted to solve the decorative dilemma, at Sway in Hampshire the structural potential of the material was realized to the full when it was stretched 218 feet into the sky. This tower was built between 1879 and 1885 in the Indo-Gothic style by Andrew Thomas Turton Peterson, a one-time High Court Judge of Calcutta. In the 1870s unemployment was rife in Hampshire and Peterson, determined upon improving the locals' lot, employed some forty unskilled labourers to build his tremendous tower. There was no scaffolding, the men worked from inside, ramming concrete into wooden frames as they rose ever higher into the sky. With the concrete hauled aloft in a bucket, by a pulley and rope dragged to and fro by a horse, the scenes on site were more reminiscent of India than of the English home counties. Judge Peterson had been touched by spiritualism during his many years in the East and this interest was rekindled by an alarming religious group 'The New Forest Shakers'. The design for his great Indian tower was guided, he claimed, by the spirit of Sir Christopher Wren who was urging him on, to build ever more in his favourite material – concrete! That Wren might have been interested in the material is, in fact, not quite as far-fetched as it seems. He always claimed that his inspiration for St Paul's had been the Pantheon in Rome which, astonishingly enough, was built of lightweight concrete in AD 127. (It was used, too, in the arches of the Colosseum.) Judge Peterson's celestial messages from Wren, imagined or otherwise, gave him the gumption – without any experience of building – to design this great Indian tower which in its day was the tallest concrete building in the world. Marching up the circular concrete stairwell of some 330 steps you are surrounded on all sides by the material, unexpectedly aligned with the Gothic windows that are slit into the walls. The good Judge also built concrete sties for his pigs, in the Moorish style for good measure.

The purists, though, were to persevere. In the 1920s and 1930s architects became entranced by concrete. They saw it as the quintessential modern material and – in an echo of Victorian debates – to build with unadorned 'honesty' became a moral crusade. We are all too well aware of the shortcomings of that crusade, although of course there are many honourable and exciting exceptions throughout Britain. 'Bendhu', a house in Northern Ireland, is one. It was self-built in the 1930s by Newton Penprase who taught art and crafts at the Belfast School of Art. The rooms were added one at a time and each one can be seen clearly outlined on the building's exterior, with them rising up, one on top of the other

Aspdin's cement works – the most palatial in the world

The concrete Pantheon of Rome AD127!

– like children's blocks – over the north Antrim coast. No better example could be found of the doctrine of 'honesty'. With its spirited and light-hearted air this little building shows that concrete need never have pulverized the passion out of architecture.

Today that tide has turned and nowhere can this be seen more dramatically than in Cambridge, where the old Addenbrooke's Hospital building – now the Judge Institute of Management Studies – has been transformed into a firework-like display of colours and contours, almost all of concrete. The architect is John Outram, whose dashingly up-to-the-minute development of this nineteenth-century building has given the material a vigorous new life and, to boot, solved all the dilemmas in the chronicles of concrete. By casting it with brick – which never loses its colour – and by inlaying it with different hues to create patterns, he has produced a truly modern method that has transformed concrete into the most multifarious of all building materials.

Meanwhile at St John's College, Oxford, Richard McCormack has resurrected the ideals of Rome while at the same time trumpeting the technology of our times. I doubt if a contemporary concrete building has ever been emblazoned with such a rich and varied mix of surfaces. Some are polished to appear as marble while others are grit blasted – leaving a powdered effect. Then there is the darkened acid-etched concrete, as well as concrete hammered and bashed with different pneumatic heads. Point chiselling has revealed the aggregate, giving a rustication intentionally similar to the base of the neo-classical Ashmolean Museum nearby. 'Concrete is too important a material to be hidden away or camouflaged for artistic reasons,' says McCormack. 'We have got to find the language of the material again, using it boldly and honestly.'

So, not before time, it's a hearty huzzah for concrete!

St John's College, Oxford, a celebration of concrete

DORSET'S DELIGHT

Bournemouth!
How shall I sing thy praise, fair favoured spot,
That nestles 'mid thy hills and silvery groves
Of fragrant pines? From out thy dense alcoves,
Bright villas peep – 't has been my happy lot
To dwell amid thy shady nooks, I wot,
Through many winters.

(below) The beauties of Bournemouth

These words were happily honed by Sir Merton Russell Cotes who, with his 'beloved and darling' wife Annie, was to leave his strangely wonderful house, East Cliff Hall, along with its outlandish contents and elegant art gallery, to the City of Bournemouth. The house is remarkable in that it is a unique survival in the British Isles of the middling monied merchant's style, where every inch was a swell one. Throughout the land, from Ealing to

The Royal Bath Hotel, Bournemouth
(Facade & Grounds overlooking the sea)

Edinburgh, there were houses like this, crammed and coated with splendour by nineteenth-century burghers. Now they have all gone – gutted and geared up to new roles as nursing homes, flats and guest-houses. Stately homes have survived by the score, as has many a manor of 'the middle size' and terraces and the tenements, too; but you can no longer see the particular overblown opulence of the local business big-wig. The only way you can relish it nowadays – at least in this country – is in the movies, with stars such as Ingrid Bergman enveloped by its glories in *Gaslight*. In the United States, however, such nineteenth-century bourgeois swagger does still thrive. Whereas in Britain conservationists have concentrated, for the most part, on preserving the architecture of the aristocrats, in America they have concentrated on preserving the homes of merchant princes – their great past. Hence the singularity of East Cliff Hall. It looks for all the world like a robber baron's mansion from a Midwestern state that has floated across the Atlantic to be grounded on Bournemouth's shore.

This was a resort which according to the Russell Coteses was 'a water of the first order' and he and his wife were tireless in their promotion of the town. 'Never say see Naples and Die; rather see Bournemouth and Live!' was their cry as they soldiered on, forever building and beautifying the resort in all manner of ways, to the 'rapturous approval' of its citizens. 'When I first came to Bournemouth it was *terra incognita*', wrote Sir Merton, 'and I determined to make it the talk of Europe.' He wrote two exhaustingly heavy – both in style and weight – volumes of an autobiography, *Home and Abroad*, that turgidly trudged through his every triumph. Each letter he wrote and received is recorded, all published paeans of praise – and there were many – and every word uttered on the public platform, down to 'Loud applause' and 'Hearty cheers'.

a violin'. They made a mournful mission to Cawnpore where they talked to an eyewitness of the massacre of 1857 and inspected every melancholy bullet mark from the seige at Lucknow, marvelling all the while at the heroism of so many of the 'delicately nurtured ladies'. Their guide was a 'young Hindu with a

The Russell Coteses in the Royal Bath Hotel (below) with (left) their riches to the roof at East Cliff Hall

Two distinctly different men emerge: one an upright self-adulating snob who when courting the company of royalty 'personally realised the depth of the Prince of Wales' genial temperament' and the other an adventurous spirit who would go shark fishing in Australia; one whose narrow mind would ooze out such vituperations as '*MIRABILE DICTU* … girls are now bathing with men in skin tights at fashionable watering places', while the other wrote merrily of the rustling of snakes eating rats and mice under his bed in Ceylon.

Sir Merton and Lady Russell Cotes travelled widely. 'What do they know of England, who only England know' was a much-used quotation. But however adventurous their foreign forays, for them Bournemouth was best. Their wanderings are woven into the very fabric of the house, giving it an extra air of the exotic. India emerges in a tiny Mogul chamber designed to remind them of their visit to the Taj Mahal by moonlight, accompanied by 'an officer with

delightfully mellifluous Irish brogue – a very novel feature!'

Their adventures can be traced throughout the house. There is a tiny envelope, for example, containing 'Volcanic dust' that was plucked by Sir Merton from the jaws of scalding death – 'a surging, rolling, splashing, tossing sea of molten fire' – in a volcanic crater in Hawaii. The Russell Coteses had been guests in Hawaii of 'The Right Honourable Archibald Cleghorn and his wife, The Princess Like Like'. Another souvenir was a small volume, *Sanitary*

'The Lancashire witch', 'the Laughing Cavalier' et al

The splendours of the Henry Irving shrine

Instructions for Hawaiians, by The Right Honourable W.M. Gibson – 'a most admirable treatise' wrote Sir Merton.

They seemed to shed all convention when travelling, writing cheerily of Burma, where 'home life was lively rather than agreeable, with a showerbath of insect carcases, including a green moth with a twelve inch wing span falling on our food whilst dining one night'. They preserved a taxidermist's menagerie from foreign parts giving pride of place to the kea, a now-extinct sheep-eating parrot from New Zealand which was quite rightly considered a great rarity. Having developed a liking for the suet around a sheep's kidney, the bird would bore its beak through the animal's back and fly off replenished, leaving the rest of the carcass intact!

Other delights in the house include 'Art as applied to Feathers' from Rio de Janeiro and a model of wrestlers from Japan that caused the actress Sarah Bernhardt 'to go into raptures' when she came to tea.

'She possessed a marvellously virile and versatile nature,' wrote Sir Merton, 'full of emotional pathos, which can be roused to the highest pitch of vehement violence, making a very affectionate friend or a very bitter enemy.' They had met through Sir Henry Irving, a life-long friend, to whom a shrine was built in East Cliff Hall. His bronze bust gleams forth in a pink room, gilded with mottoes and filled with objects from Irving's life. The great actor's make-up box is there, all in disarray, with the rouge that was powdered on to those fine features. Locks of his hair lie beside his death mask, and there is a quantity of stage props, such as the skull held by Irving as Hamlet, with 'his princely air, his tenderness and his power of suggesting doom'.

The importance of Bournemouth is proclaimed throughout East Cliff Hall, indeed the art gallery was built specially for the town. 'Without art mankind would be in a deplorable condition,' wrote Sir Merton, who set up an excellent scheme whereby people could borrow his paintings to hang on their walls. His taste in art was not universally acclaimed, with *Dawn of Love* by William Etty causing an outcry. 'It is of no moral value', thundered one enraged critic, 'but if it were a prelude to a night's debauchery, I would consider it the best oil painting of its kind… In civilised life the dawn of love is not heralded with clothes off!' There were rich ripostes: 'If your critic – no doubt with shares in some clothing company – objects to love coming into the world unclothed, let him by prayer and supplication persuade our Maker to engage a tailor!'

When Mayor and Mayoress of Bournemouth, the Russell Coteses were lavish in their duties. In 1895 they gave a fancy dress party for several hundred children and a sumptuous album survives of the proceedings. Embossed like an illuminated manuscript, it is filled with photographs of the many 'picturesque and charming costumes' such as a 'Lancashire Witch' and 'Robin Redbreast'.

Lady Russell Cotes, or 'The Queen of Bournemouth' as she was lovingly called, died in 1920. Sir Merton died nine months later and was buried in their mosaic-lined mausoleum, beside his wife, sixty-one years to the day after their wedding, thereby ensuring that they had never spent an anniversary apart.

The Russell Coteses worked tirelessly for their beloved town, with such schemes as promenades and a hospital, as well as parks and a winter garden, not to mention masterminding the railways to make Bournemouth only two hours from London. But their greatest act of all was to leave their remarkable house and possessions to the town. When they decided to do so, Sir Merton wrote that it made him and his wife feel 'as playful as kittens'.

Let the last words come from the Bournemouth *Observer* of 15 November 1894:

The Mayor's a man on whose importance everybody
    dotes,
Give three loud cheers for F R G S Merton Russell
    Cotes!

EASTERN

ɪᴛ is a shock and a half to come upon the Shah Jehan Mosque in Surrey. From the first glimpse of this radiant little building, with its bright white, turquoise and gold body and its gilded domes and spires – quite undimmed by the British climes – you are undoubtedly in the East, in Isfahan or Islamabad rather than down a side street in Woking. Largely paid for by the Begum Shah Jehan of Bhopal – the town now 'twinned' with Slough – the mosque was designed by W.I. Chambers and built in 1899, the first mosque in the British Isles. That it was ever constructed is thanks to a Hungarian doctor, Gottlieb Wilhelm Leitner, who had established newspapers, libraries and schools in India as well as mastering fifty languages. He became a British subject and founded an Oriental Institute in Woking, with the intention of creating an Islamic University.

Meticulous care was taken with the mosque's every detail. For example, so that the principal wall – towards which the faithful pray – would be precisely at the correct angle to Mecca, a captain of a P&O liner went to Woking and took the bearings. Inside, little yellow glass stars are pierced into the dome. The mosque was restored in 1989 – its centenary year.

The Maharajah of Benares was another patron who enhanced the home counties with Eastern exotica, with a tiny temple of an Indian well at Stoke Row in Oxfordshire – charming proof of the friendship that existed between him and Edward Anderton Reade, the Lieutenant-Governor of the North Western Provinces. When discussing the scarcity of water in Benares, Reade had once told the Maharajah of the miseries suffered in his own 'native district' in Oxfordshire; of the people being dependent on water found in dirty ponds and disused clay pits and of 'urchins being cruelly thumped by "baagins" [human tigresses] for furtive quenchings of thirst and for washing days indefinitely postponed'.

Work on the well began – at the Maharajah's request – on the Prince of Wales's wedding day in 1863. It was opened on Queen Victoria's birthday a year later. The local paper gave an ebullient account of the proceedings: 'The Nettlebed band was in great force, the crowd was enormous, and the Chiltern Hills … resounded … loudly to cheers for The Good Maharajah and his heir apparent, or the young Rajah, as the rustics shouted, from inability to give out his proper name' – which was Probhoo Sarayun.

It is a little domed temple, with a golden elephant standing atop the machinery – 'by means of which a young lad or an old woman can bring up a bucket containing nine gallons of water from three hundred and sixty-eight feet with ease and safety'. It was dug entirely by hand, by a single man in shifts –

The wonders of Woking – the Shah Jehan mosque

delving downwards more than twice the height of Nelson's Column. The Maharajah's Well at Stoke Row is now a charitable trust and kept in spanking order.

Both the Shah Jehan Mosque and the Well are rare examples of true Eastern architecture in the British Isles, unlike the kaleidoscopic display of deceits and conceits that rose up throughout the eighteenth,

nineteenth and twentieth centuries, when every conceivable type of building was clad in Eastern fancy dress. The Royal Panopticon in Leicester Square was designed by Thomas Hayter in the 'Saracenic or Moorish' style 'as a novelty'. A vast glass dome was originally planned but was sadly to be modified. Built for scientific exhibitions, as well as for promoting the arts and manufacturing, it was the proud possessor of an 'Ascending Carriage' – a little Eastern temple of an elevator that whisked the patrons aloft. A ninety foot fountain rose up to the full height of the building, past floor after floor of delights such as a 4004-piped organ with minarets. The building was disgracefully demolished in 1936. But another vision of exciting Eastern promise has been left standing – the Egyptian cinema at Sale in Cheshire, built in 1934.

Another architect, Cuthbert Brodrick, went the whole Eastern hog in Leeds when he designed the Oriental Baths in Cookridge Street in 1866. He had just completed his sturdy Corn Exchange and was able to take off on the wildest flights of architectural fancy, producing a graceful domed and minareted building in polychrome brick, encaustic tiles and terracotta.

The Egyptian style was brought to architectural attention in England by Piranesi in the mid-1700s. It reached its peak of popularity around 1810, and thereafter there were many colourful examples well into the 1930s, such as the pleasure palace of the Ritz cinema at Sale in Cheshire.

In the 1790s Joseph Gandy was proposing

Cuthbert's Brodrick's evocation of the East in Leeds

pyramids for 'pigs, poultry and their keepers' and in 1842 a Mr George Durant built just such exotica for his animals in Shropshire, with 'Scratch Before You Peck' and 'Teach Your Granny' incised into the poultry's pyramid and 'To Please The Pigs' on the porkers'.

It was Napoleon's campaigns in Egypt in 1798 that had first fuelled the fashion into a frenzied building of the style. Robert Southey wrote scathingly of all that he saw in 1807: 'The very shopboards must be

Marshall's mill, Leeds, where sheep grazed on the roof

metamorphosed into the mode, and painted in Egyptian letters which, as the Egyptians had no letters, you will doubtless conceive must be curious … with strokes of equal thickness so that those that should be thin look as if they had elephantiasis. [The Rosetta stone was not deciphered for another fifteen years.] Everything must now be Egyptian … you sit in a room hung round with mummies, and the long black lean-armed long-nosed hieroglyphical men who are enough to make the children afraid to go to bed.'

Craven Cottage in Fulham had one such interior: it was built in the 1780s for Lady Craven – later the

Craven Cottage, the site of Fulham football ground

Margravine of Anspach – a dramatist and composer of musical farces as well as an authoress of such works as *A Tale for Christmas, Modern Anecdotes of the Family of Kinvervankotsprakengatchdern*. Horace Walpole gives an account of her after a performance in Drury Lane: 'There is such an integrity and frankness in her consciousness of her own beauty and talents, that she speaks of them with a "naivete" as if she had no property in them, but only wore them as gifts of the gods'. She even went so far as to call her autobiography, *The Beautiful Lady Craven*. In 1805 she leased Craven Cottage to Walsh Porter, an art dealer, who, with Thomas Hopper the architect, created an Egyptian extravaganza behind the rustic exterior. The room

Devonport – from eastern erudition to Jamaican jam sessions

was copied from one of Denon's illustrations, made during Bonaparte's campaigns in Egypt, and no detail was spared; the ceiling, emblazoned with hieroglyphics, was supported by four slender palms with carved drooping foliage and then there were eight hearty columns – also covered with hieroglyphics – that rose up the full height of the room. A life-size 'movable camel' was part of the arrangements as well as an immense bronze woman holding a curtain of imitation tiger skin. The windows were all tapered in the Pharaonic style, as were the doors – sturdy enough to do credit to a cemetery entrance – with

their massive and intricately carved surrounds. Going through one, flanked by sphinxes, you found yourself in a sixty-foot gothic gallery painted in imitation of Henry VII's chapel at Westminster. Through the other, flanked by mummies, you walked into a 'Tartar or Saracen chieftain's tent' hung with mirrors and blue-striped canvas and lit with a crescent window. Craven Cottage was burnt to the ground in 1888, by tramps sheltering in the then empty house. Fulham Football Ground now stands on the site.

A correspondent in *Ackermann's Repository* of 1810 was a scornful critic of attempts to evoke the East in the British Isles: 'Such absurdities might afford pastime to youth, but are beneath the dignity of real taste; and persons of fortune, desirous of acquiring the reputation of possessing that quality, cannot be too careful to avoid them.' Luckily such contempt – and there was plenty of it – went unheeded. The Egyptian Hall was built in Piccadilly in 1812, cocking a stylish snook at such sneers. It was designed by P.F. Robinson, who had worked on Brighton Pavilion. The building was demolished in 1905 and Piccadilly is the poorer for that.

Not so Penzance, however, where the Egyptian House built in 1835 – as an almost exact copy of its London counterpart – still stands. Bought and restored by the Landmark Trust in 1973, it was subtly repainted in the 1980s. Robinson may well have had a hand in its design, but in the main it was created by a local architect, John Foulston. An ardent classicist, he even went so far as to thunder round Cornwall in a chariot. His partner architect George Wightwick left a pleasing description: 'The vehicle which served him as a gig, was built in the form of an antique "biga", or

Egyptian promise at Sale in Cheshire

war-chariot; with a seat furtively smuggled into the service of comfort, though he ascended from it from behind with true classical orthodoxy and looked (as far as his true English face and costume allowed) like Ictinus of the Parthenon "out for a lark".' Foulston was responsible for the Egyptian library in Devonport – now a bitter-sweet tale of our times: he designed a picturesque group – a classical temple of a town hall and a 'Hindoo' Nonconformist chapel as well as the fanciful Egyptian library – all set down amidst Corinthian-columned terraces, today a swathe of 1960s flats of the grimmest and greyest order. The temple still survives, as does the library – brightly blazing forth in new and suitably high-spirited colours. It is a club, with such attractions as 'Jamaican Jam Sessions'. Inside, pinball and Coca-Cola machines jostle with the Egyptian detailing but the building is safe, sound and richly appreciated.

In 1840, John Marshall, pioneer of the Leeds flax industry, commissioned Ignatius Bonomi to design an Egyptian temple to house his new mill. The fact that the ancient Egyptians produced quantities of flax for their linen was the scholarly reason for his scheme – it was more than just a fashionable fancy. Then the largest mill in Europe (and the founding influence for the flax industry in Belfast), the building caused a sensation. It is truly massive – covering two acres – and must have seemed all the more so when built in its originally rural surroundings. Columns with papyrus-flowered capitals loom forth and serpents support winged suns. Beneath the ornamental coved frieze there are a thousand smiling serpents. A surprise of equal measure was to be found on the roof, where Marshall added extra romance by sowing a green meadow which he filled with sheep. It was 'luxuriant grass', according to the *Penny Magazine* of 1843, 'with slight undulations of level as to make the resemblance to a field more striking'. Sixty-five

Here lies Lord Kilmorey, in a dressing gown of rat's fur

pyramid fanlights – illuminating the mill below – stood in these bizarrely rural surroundings 'inducing one to ponder whether any gardening operations are going on'. Drainage was organized down the sixty pillars supporting the roof of the mill. This happy arrangement was abandoned when a sheep fell through a skylight into the spinning machinery, although one 'noble lord' at Westminster suggested that 'such mills allowing cultivation on the roof would be important in future agricultural development'.

The 'Millocrat' Marshall built schools, a library and a church for his workers, but employed children under tyrannical conditions. Some were as young as six and 500 were under fifteen. If they dozed off their heads were plunged into a cistern of icy water and if they slacked they had to stand on a stool, on one leg, holding a heavy bar at arm's length above their heads for as long as half an hour. The 'Radical Rhymster' was moved to write, 'These are the children all forlorn, who toil and slave from night till morn, in spinning the flax, all heckled and torn, that lays in the house that Jack built.'

In south London there is an example of Egyptian architecture that can only be seen from the top of a double decker bus. Trundling along, between Edwardian and 1920s houses, you suddenly spot it; over a high wall there is a glimpse of Egypt, in a tiny green and overgrown plot of land. It is the perfect pink and grey granite mausoleum that was built by the Earl of Kilmorey for his beloved mistress Priscilla Host, in 1850. Designed by Kendall, the little Egyptian temple was erected in Brompton Cemetery. Twelve years later it was moved, to stand in the grounds of the Earl's new house, Woburn Park in Chertsey. After only five years it was off again, this time to Gordon House in Twickenham – already owned by the Earl – to which he moved back in 1868. Wherever he went, so his mistress went too, in her smoothly splendent home. From when the mausoleum was first built there was a space beside her, ready for the Earl's remains. For twenty-six years there had been a coffin as well – covered with crimson velvet – in which he would often lie when rehearsing his own funeral. There was an underground tunnel between the little temple and the house and 'when in the mood' – according to the *Isleworth Citizen* – 'he would summon his servants, dress in a white garb, and proceed to the mausoleum'. When he finally expired, aged ninety-two, he was buried in a dressing gown of rats' fur.

There is of course Oriental architecture in abundance throughout Britain, too, but there is no space here to spout of its splendours – save to say that the 1760s Chinese Room at Claydon House in Buckinghamshire, with its carvings by Luke Lightfoot, is more magical than most. With a feast of woodwork, all painted white, it is like whipped cream or icing sugar, making you want to lick your lips at its sheer delectability. At the time of writing, funds are being raised to rebuild the circa eighteenth-century Chinese House at Stowe in Buckinghamshire, in the memory of my dear friend Gervase Jackson Stops who died in 1995.

A Lightfooted fantasy at Claydon

FUN DAYS OUT

INCE the early 1730s Blackpool has been an ever-growing feast of fun – a mammoth *mille-feuille* of merriment, with delight upon delectable delight added over the years. From the first visitors who enjoyed the health-giving pleasure of drinking the prescribed dose of twenty-five gallons of sea water – a pint at a time – to the roaring terror of today's roller-coaster, Blackpool has provided ever more fantastical and frenzied entertainment to attract the crowds. In the 1890s a particularly outlandish scheme was devised when a hundred parrots, trained to screech about the delights of the Winter Gardens, were left in hotels and restaurants all over Lancashire. They had plenty to screech about. The word 'Progress' is the town's motto and in its pursuit of novel pleasure Blackpool can never rest upon its larky laurels. Much has been lost in this headlong rush, but much remains – tiny and tremendous traces of the town's ever-changing face. For over a hundred years there have been two main centres of entertainment in Blackpool: the Tower and the Winter Gardens, both of them built with the art and architecture of fantasy.

Most tremendous of all – and it would be hard to find a more opulent spot in the British Isles – is the Tower Ballroom, commissioned by John Bickerstaffe in 1899 in the florid French Renaissance style of Frank Matcham, king of theatrical design. Like a giantess's boudoir upholstered in gold, tiers of boxes bulge forth amongst the glitter, swelling on up to the ceiling where a pageant of plasterwork surrounds paintings of celestial scenes – one with an alarming devil embracing flower-bedecked maidens. 'BID ME DISCOURSE AND I WILL ENCHANT THINE EAR' is emblazoned over the proscenium arch. One terrible morning, on 14 December 1956, this stupendous room was gutted by a fire, caused, it is said, by a single cigarette. With inspired grandiosity Douglas Bickerstaffe – 'hewn of the same granite as his father' – decreed that the ballroom be entirely rebuilt to its original designs. And so it was – every last gleaming inch of it – down to the 75,000 blocks of mahogany, oak, maple and walnut on the dance floor. (They had already been replaced in 1933, when the quantity of dancers had worn the floor away by five-eighths of an inch.)

On a busy night in the 1930s as many as six thousand people might have been capering, under the guidance – 'this way round, this way round' – of one, two or even three masters of ceremonies. After three turns on the floor you were told to leave for 'a fresh look about'. Laurel and Hardy entertained here, as did Duke Ellington, Arthur Askey and, of course, the late, great 'Mr Blackpool Himself', Reginald Dixon, who would sit at his Wurlitzer on the podium

The Tower Ballroom – a giantess's gilded boudoir

surrounded by a forest of palm trees. In 1910 the draw of the day was 'Little Emmie Tweedsdale', otherwise known as 'the Petit Pavlova', to whom time must have been kind as she was still billed as 'Little Emmie' in 1935. The Spinsters' Ball was a regular feature with rose petals showering down on the dancers. During the war the ballroom was given over to silk parachute-making with, at one point, Dame Clara Butt giving the workers her stentorian rendition of 'Land of Hope and Glory'. Years later, during a victory ball, the ballroom was gatecrashed by wounded veterans, who were cheered to the gilded rafters.

Blackpool's second centre of gaiety is the Spanish Hall in the Winter Gardens with whole villages sprouting out from the balconies on the walls and lights blazing forth from every window. This was all created by Andrew Mazzei, chief designer at Gaumont Studios in the 1930s. There are pleasing details from Blackpool's past throughout the Winter Gardens: late nineteenth-century tiled tableaux of merbabies as well as 1930s chandeliers that have been wrought into crowing cockerels. Gaudí-esque ceramics streak up stairways and plaster figures of 'antique distinction' enhance the walls of the main concourse. Then there is the ornate Pavilion Theatre, where Sarah Bernhardt played in 1882, giving a distressingly inaudible performance in French to yells of 'SPEAK UP, LASS!'

Hidden away amid the grim ruination of what were once the Winter Gardens, you find one of the most important of all decorative details in Blackpool; a life-size ceramic woman standing in an area jam-packed with pipes and meters. She is part of the grand array of tiles that flanked the entrance to the Empress Ballroom – there were once twenty-eight such

Emily Neatby, banished to a boiler room

The North Pier, the first of three to be built in Blackpool, was designed in 1862–3 by Eugenius Birch. In the late 1800s and early 1900s both religious services and 'sacred concerts' were held every Sunday to assuage the guilt of the Sabbath revellers. They took place on the pier in the Eastern Pavilion – sadly destroyed by fire – which had been built for 'conversation, sewing, keeping a rendezvous or any other kindred "kill-time" occupations for the sea-side lounger'. This had risen up in fierce competition with the Winter Gardens which could boast of an 'Indian Lounge' and a 'Fairyland'. These in turn were in racing rivalry with such other attractions as the Opera House, a bear pit and boxing kangaroos, not to mention the disgraced Vicar of Stiffkey, who had been accused of consorting with fallen women and protested his innocence by publicly starving, first in a large barrel and then in a glass-topped cabinet, with people paying two pence a time to come and gawp at the sight.

Then of course there was the Tower, the beacon of Blackpool that was built in 1896 – the season that boomed to bursting point. One visitor from Burnley found the sitting room of his lodging house so full of visitors that there was room neither to sit nor stand. His bedroom had been let to a honeymoon couple and he was forced to share with nine bachelors with only three beds between them. The order of the night was 'Two stout men and one not-so-fat to each bed, with the stout parties on either side. We were laid like spoons, and it was impossible to turn until one of us had given the signal – then we all had to turn at once.' The Tower – then the tallest building in the kingdom – was the main attraction welcoming the world and his wife to Blackpool. Its four Eiffel

beauties in arched niches. W.J. Neatby, famed for his Art Nouveau ceramics, was responsible and it is said that this is his wife, Emily, of whom he was so jealous that he kept her locked in their house with the blinds permanently drawn. More of these fine figures are boarded up in a shoe shop and it is hoped that they will soon be restored.

Tower-like legs are hidden within a Victorian build-ing, where they shelter, of all surprises, a magical Mogul circus. The ring is dead centre beneath the Tower, its surroundings the richest Eastern exotica, all ablaze with gold leaf. The Tower's great iron and steel structure can clearly be seen, sweeping up and arching round from the legs that seem to taper down on all four corners. But it is the circus's grand finale

The 1930s casino swooping into the future

which best evokes Blackpool's sense of flamboyance; a triumph of Victorian taste and technology which has been kept in startlingly smooth working order for one hundred years. Defying the evidence before your eyes, the circus ring sinks and in sixty seconds flat is filled with 40,000 gallons of water for a dazzling aquatic act. There are no longer any animals in the circus but their curious quarters still survive beneath the ring today and the faintest sense of them too – in the nostrils.

Since the 1930s there has been a solid core of architectural excellence in Blackpool – along the 'Golden Mile' at the Pleasure Beach, where Joseph Emberton was commissioned by Leonard Thompson to design a number of dashing buildings to give an identity and order to the place. They are masterly examples of the 'Moderne Movement' of the 1930s – smooth, suave and curvilinear, it was the style that gave such hope for a streamlined future. The Casino in Blackpool has two swirling staircase towers with a cafeteria that sweeps the full half circle of the building. Emberton was responsible, too, for the 'Fun House' which was burnt to the ground in 1991. He designed the 'Ice Drome' as well as the 'Grand National' rollercoaster, another 'Moderne' landmark which has recently been restored. He built a private flat for the Thompson family, who still own and run the Pleasure Beach which survives in pristine order. Mrs Doris Thompson, now in her nineties, continues to come to the Pleasure Beach every day. She can remember Joseph Emberton's extreme absentmindedness. For example, he left all his architectural drawings on the train. He had an especially sweet tooth and would be forever scurrying off to satisfy his cravings with candy floss. The first time he tasted Lancashire Hot Pot, he took three helpings, followed by treacle pudding and cheese.

There are other architectural landmarks at the Pleasure Beach and these rides have been given 'Historic Markers'. Noah's Ark was built in the 1920s and the River Caves date from 1904. They have a most surprising structural secret. When they needed to be repaired after the Second World War material was in short supply and they were reroofed with the scrapped 'Mulberry Harbours' – the inventions that made possible the liberation of Europe in 1944 – and pontoon bridges used for crossing the Rhine. The oldest ride of all is the Hiram Maxim Flying Machine, built in 1904, and designed by Sir Hiram S. Maxim as a way of making money for his attempts to be the first man to fly the measured mile. (In the end his steam-driven machine was deemed too heavy to leave the ground.) His machinery at Blackpool, however, has remained in constant use for ninety years.

Sir Hiram was a self-styled inventor. Born and brought up in a bear-infested forest in Maine, he was awarded the Légion d'honneur for his innovations with electric lighting, as well as knighted for devising the first automatic machine gun – initially sold to the Chinese as a way of felling trees. On the maiden voyage of Blackpool's Flying Machine it was said that there was 'an irresistible desire to cheer' as 'the enormous crowds made the air dizzy with their laughter and other manifestations of delight'.

Today Blackpool can boast of having 'The Big One' – the tallest and fastest roller-coaster in the world – built in 1994 by Geoffrey Thompson, grandson of the Pleasure Beach's founder.

With such a rich appreciation of the past, the present and the future, Blackpool, rest assured, will be forever festively abreast of the times.

GLAZED GLORIES

HE art of tile decoration spread like wildfire over the buildings of Britain in the last half of the nineteenth century. A shining proof of the newly industrialized age, buildings great and small were coated in its gloss. Tiles were designed to beautify the walls and floors of churches and public houses as well as public lavatories. Hospitals were covered with ceramic surfaces – most excitingly in the children's wards – as were town halls and innumerable shops, even stately homes. The heart of the humblest house was incomplete without the decorative tile glinting from around the hearth. The ceramic tile was affordable art and it reflected Britain's new affluence.

Today, after half a century of perplexing neglect and destruction, its popularity is once again assured. Tiles of every description can be found in high street shops. Firms which have thrived on the bland blankness of their designs during the 1950s, 1960s and 1970s are producing elaborately embellished ceramics once again. New and innovative firms are flourishing and many of the richest nineteenth-century designs are actually being remade.

There were none more splendid than 'The South Kensington Alphabet' of the 1870s, designed for the Refreshment Rooms of the South Kensington Museum – now the Victoria and Albert – the first museum restaurant in the country. The tiles are massive – 26cm x 30cm – and richly designed with figures and letters in satisfying sculptured relief: a boy and a snake grapple with E and there is a winged cherub with a watering can who walks through D. The letter B supports a falconer with his hawk. They were designed for the Centre Room, one of three refreshment rooms that were smothered with tiles. The alphabet, as elaborate as it is, was a mere detail in the room's overall design, which has amorini dancing round the dado and majolica camels and elephants framing mirrors, surrounded on all sides by ceramic walls and pillars. The letters, designed by Godfrey Sykes – whose modest back-view self-portrait leans on I – are at picture-rail level. Marching round, they read from Ecclesiastes:'THERE IS NOTHING BETTER FOR A MAN THAN THAT HE SHOULD EAT AND DRINK AND THAT HE SHOULD MAKE HIS SOUL ENJOY GOOD IN HIS LABOUR XYZ.' Not surprisingly, with all its elaboration, a visitor in 1870 said that he needed several drinks before he could decipher it.

Today, thanks to the wondrous turnabout in taste, these are again being manufactured. I myself had an even better scheme for my sitting room in which every letter is woven into the words: 'ZEAL FOR LIFE BEAUTY FOOD JOY OF HOME WITH KINDSHIP OF

The curious creatures of Walter Crane

COMPANIONS PURE LOVE OF EXQUISITE DOGS'. Sadly though, it was too costly to contemplate. Furthermore, anyone trying to read it would have to be blind drunk, as a plain tile – with a dot – that originally went between the words, is no longer made.

Herbert Minton was responsible for the first boom of the tile business in Britain and it was he, too, who revived the long-lost art of ecclesiastical encaustic tiling which had died with the Reformation. In 1843 he showed off his wares to the Society of Arts; 'at a brilliant gathering, at which were present Prince Albert, the Duke of Wellington, Sir Robert Peel, a number of Bishops and about thirty foreign Princes'. All of them were captivated, Prince Albert ordering a 'decorated pavement' for Osborne and Sir Robert Peel probably influencing the decision to cover the floors of the new Houses of Parliament with Minton tiles, designed by Pugin.

In 1858 Queen Victoria and Prince Albert commissioned Minton to adorn a dairy at Windsor, which had been designed by the Prince as part of his agricultural improvements of the Home Farm. It is a bejewelled beauty of a room where a pin could not be pricked between the decoration. Tiny oranges, their leaves entwined with blue and white ribbons, weave about the walls. Ceramic roundels of the Queen, her consort and their children are held aloft by seahorses whilst V & A medallions are supported by dolphins. Babies prance through majolica tableaux of seasonal pastimes – ploughing with goats and dancing round the maypole as well as gathering in the harvest with goat carts – two Minton fountains, one of a merman, the other a mermaid, are held aloft by arum lilies and bulrushes, water lilies and cranes. Behind all this flamboyance is the Prince's practicality. The dairy is air-conditioned by a paddle that draws oil-light fumes out through the pierced ceiling tiles. There is a rabbit warren of pipes beneath the floor to keep everything cool.

Elihu Burritt, the American consul in Birmingham, otherwise known as 'The Learned Blacksmith' – he had started in that trade and mastered fifty-seven languages – visited the dairy in 1865 and left a pearl of purple prose: 'The Queen's Dairy! How Saxon and homelike sounds that term! … The Queen herself, in straw bonnet … dropping happy and smiling looks into pails and pans of milk and cream. The Queen's Dairy! The very name seems to link her queenhood to the happiest and homeliest experiences of rural life; to attach her, by a sensible lien of industrial sympathy, to all the farmers' wives in the British Empire … The milk room … is perfection itself … polished after the similitude of a palace. The walls, the long marble tables, the fountains, the statuary of rustic life, and all the finely sculpted allegories look as if wrought from new milk petrified just as the cream begins to rise to the surface … No description I could give would convey any adequate idea of the refined taste, fertile genius and exquisite art brought to bear upon this little palace.'

There is a mere bathroom of the same palatial order at Gledhow Hall in Leeds. Rich in architectural faïence work by Burmantofts of Leeds, as much attention has been paid to the ceiling as to the walls and fireplace. It was built by the industrialist politician James Kitson in 1885 as part of his aggrandizement of the house in which he entertained week in and week out for six months of every year. When guests arrived they would sweep up an uncommonly long and curving drive, despite the back of the house being bang on the road. For Lord Rosebery's visit it was lined with 200 torch bearers. Prime Minister Gladstone was also a constant visitor and no doubt disported himself in the bath, as indeed must have every Liberal prime minister who stayed there until Kitson's death in 1911. Although Gledhow is now surrounded almost up to its walls by blocks of flats, the bathroom, I am happy to say, survives. A quantity of such ornate bathrooms are still going strong at 8 Addison Road in London. Their tiles were produced by one of the greatest of all ceramicists, William de Morgan. There are designs of leaping rats as well as of owls catching mice by the tail. A pelican gazes at a frog and a fox carries off his trophy of a goose, as does an otter with a fish.

Tiles of a very different type are to be found in the City of London, in the charmingly named Postman's Park that was planted out in the early 1900s for postmen to enjoy a bit of peace. What at first appears to be an extended pergola is in fact a 'memorial cloister' – a fifty-foot-long roofed-over gallery of tiled tablets recording tales of self-sacrifice. It was conceived by the painter G.F. Watts, who announced that in honour of Queen Victoria's jubilee there should be a memorial to the heroes of everyday life. In a letter to *The Times* in 1887 he wrote: 'The character of a Nation, as

GLEDHOW HALL. LEEDS.
J. Kitson Junr Esqre
BATH-ROOM IN BURMANTOFT FAIENCE.
Messrs Chorley and Connon.
Architects.

Wyman & Sons Photo-Litho.

G? Queen St London W.C.

A frenzy of faience

a people of great deeds, is one that should never be lost sight of. It must surely be a matter of regret that names worthy to be remembered and stories stimulating and instructive are allowed to be forgotten.' He cited the bravery of Alice Ayres, '...a maid of all work, who saved her master's three children from a blazing house'. Because the idea was not taken up, Watts built the cloister at his own expense – arranging for thirteen tablets to be displayed. After his death Mrs Watts put up another thirty-four and yet another was added in 1930. They show the perilous tale of Arthur Strange and Mark Tomlinson, 'who on a desperate venture to save two girls from quicksand in Lincolnshire, were themselves engulfed'. Then there was Davis Selves who, aged twelve, 'supported his drowning playfellow and sank with him clasped in his arms – September 12th 1886'.

Strolling down the Strand nearby, and diverted by the dignity of the Law Courts, you could easily miss the seemingly bejewelled entrance to what was once the Royal Courts of Justice Restaurant, now Lloyds Bank. Like an exotic courtyard it is an entrance that befitted a restaurant described as 'the handsomest and most elegant in London'. There are swathes of ceramics – all in Doulton ware – weaving and twisting around columns as well as encrusting the walls with gem-like protuberances. In its heyday two fountains played beneath flying fish, with the water churning up from a 250-foot deep artisan well.

This was originally the site of the Palsgrave Head, a

tavern built in 1615 where the playwright Ben Jonson would often come to quaff. He was to be duly honoured in 1883 when tiled tableaux of his plays were set into the panelled walls of the new restaurant. They alternate with an array of ceramic chrysanthemums and other fruits and flowers in elegant pots – all named from those grown in the Temple Gardens in the nineteenth century: 'Fair Maid of Guernsey' and the 'Common Cucumber'. The restaurant had what was described as 'the very novel feature ... the same air conditioning used for ships' saloons!' In fact, astonishingly, their ventilation system seems to have been manned by two women pedalling away on a tandem bicycle connected to giant bellows in a windowless room deep down in the basement. Day in and day out – in shifts – they strenuously rode on, as air gushed from little hinged mahogany panels among the tiled tableaux in the restaurant. The rusting skeleton of the bicycle is still testimony to their slave labour today. It is thought to have been invented by Dan T. Albone and a tempting description of its uses was published in *Bicycling News* on 18 March 1888: '... no family should be without it. It converts into a Safety or Tandem for the road, into a lunch basket or foot warmer on the rail, a life belt or a lobster pot for those at sea, and a garden roller, hat rack or fire stove ornament for domestic use.' This fails to mention its air-conditioning powers – put to such alarming use below stairs, for the benefit of unwitting clients in the tile-encased restaurant above.

(Loved Ones) The shrine to Hoover the poodle, arranged and shown off by his master David Harrison in the flat that they shared together at Bow in the East End of London. Hoover's ashes are in a china musical poodle. Overall a gilded hand belonging to Jayne Mansfield – 'the patron saint of poodles' – gathers his soul up to a polystyrene heaven. Hoover's portrait blazes bright, surrounded by gilded cherubs, while a puce 'Venus de Poodle' stands by a golden box of tissues 'for crying over the sad affair'.

above and left The most beautiful parish library in Britain, dating from 1623 and hidden away within the walls of the church of St Mary the Virgin in the suburbs of Slough. Built by Sir John Kidderminster in 1623, it is reached only by walking through an ornately pinnacled pew. Framed grisaille cartouches cover the walls from floor to ceiling, with the apostles, as well as prophets and fathers of the church, all painted in brilliant hues. (Zeta).

right The charms of new concrete, wrought with modern methods into dramatic new colours and contours by the architect John Outram at the Judge Institute of Managment Studies – the old Addenbrooke's Hospital building – in Cambridge (Concrete).

above (Heathrow) Sandwiched between the airport and the M4 motorway, Elizabeth Countess of Berkeley lies on her tomb in St Dunstan's Church at Cranford. She was sculpted by Nicholas Stone in Bernini's workshop in Rome. It has even been said that the great master lent his own hand.

left (Isle of Bute) The splendours of the great hall at Mount Stuart on the Island of Bute that was built by the 3rd Marquess of Bute between 1879 and 1900. Walls and pillars of rarest marble and alabaster shoot up to a vaulted ceiling that is emblazoned with the constellations and with mirrored stars glimmering amongst figures of the zodiac. The colours of the stained glass windows are splashed throughout, with their zodiacal and mythological forms charging round amid waves of purple, scarlet, blue and green.

above Devils boil murderers in cauldrons in one of the rarest wall paintings in Europe, a mere mile from the M25. Dating from 1200, this Last Judgement is as grisly as it is glorious. It decorated the whitewashed walls of the church of St Peter and St Paul at Chaldon in Surrey (M25).

right (Art Nouveau) These writhing forms embrace the Duke of Clarence's tomb in the Albert Chapel at Windsor. Created by Alfred Gilbert, this giant jewel with figures of silver and bronze, gold and aluminium, took him thirty-six tormented years to finish. The chapel was set a'shimmering in 1869 by George Gilbert Scott, with marbles and mosaics by Triqueti, but Alfred Gilbert was to beat this splendour at its own game.

The hauntingly horrible Malay model of a man with an abundance of ginger sprouting hair is one of the hundreds of curiositites to be found in Kinloch Castle. The house was built by Sir George Bullough in 1901 for two stalking months a year and has remained with every inch of its Edwardian opulence intact – smothered throughout with magnificent and monstrous paraphernalia of the period (Rhum).

HEATHROW

To be in Heathrow Airport is to be in the historic bosom of the British Isles. With its 'pure sweet air of antiquity … in interest it is un-approachable in the land.' So wrote a Mr J. Pendral Brodhurst in the 1930s when Hounslow Heath was still asleep.

Where sloping glades extend their lengthening lines,
Where nature dressed in gay disorder shines.

What is so extraordinary is that, to a large extent, the same can still be said of Heathrow today. Rural and architectural miracles of survival remain around the entire perimeter – within yards of the runways – and a cannon, marking the first inch measured for the Ordnance Survey by General Roy, on 17 August 1784, stands bang in the middle of the airport. This inaugural ceremony was one of the great spectacles of the day, with George III no less, coming to marvel. Never before had there been an attempt both to measure and map the British Isles.

Within spitting distance of the world's biggest airport there are no fewer than five villages – Stanwell, Harlington, Harmondsworth, Cranford and Bedfont – full of sixteenth-, seventeenth-, eighteenth- and nineteenth-century buildings and complete with ancient churches. All of them are peopled, as is the airport, with as rich a roll call of ghosts as can be imagined. What a sight and a half it would make if they all assembled together on the tarmac: Lord Knyvett who foiled the Gunpowder Plot lies buried beneath a magnificent marble monument in Stanwell Church, only yards from Runway 5 to the south; while to the north at Harmondsworth Richard Cox who propagated the first Cox's Orange Pippin is buried. Nicholas Hilliard, the great seventeenth-century miniaturist, lived at Poyle Manor, with 'lawns of living velvet' and Nell Gwyn lived on the heath at Greshams Farm. Eustace Burneby patented the first white writing paper at Stanwell in 1675 and Isambard Kingdom Brunel lived at Cranford. They will join a good crowd: legions of Romans who settled on the heath between 500 and 300 BC and built a temple on the site of the main runway; then King John who celebrated the signing of the Magna Carta with a tournament on these flatlands with a bear as chief prize. After that came Oliver Cromwell with his 20,000 men, who waited on Hounslow Heath before marching in triumph to London to take over King, Parliament and country, Charles I having himself camped there when John Evelyn recorded seeing 'new sorts of soldiers called grenadiers'. Most glittering of all, though, were the camps set up by James II, in 1685–8, to which thousands flocked, as if to a fair. According to

Macaulay: 'Mingled with the musketeers and dragoons was a multitude of fine gentlemen and ladies from Whitefriars, invalids in sedans ... lackeys in rich liveries.' It is said that all the commanders 'profusely vied with one another as to who had the most expensive and magnificent tent'.

Individuals of startling note add their own colourful strands to Heathrow's web of history: Robert de Salis who rode in the Charge of the Light Brigade and who is buried at Harlington; Sir John Suckling, the inventor of cribbage, who lived on Hounslow Heath in the 1600s. Jonathan Swift read the final chapter of *Gulliver's Travels* out loud for the first time to his friends, the writers Alexander Pope, John Dryden and John Gay, at Lord Bolingbroke's house, Dawley Farm, which stood on a site but yards from Runway 8 at Harlington. To give his stately pile a rural air, Bolingbroke had painted the walls of his hall with a vast array of rakes and spades, as well as 'prongs and other implements of husbandry as one might see arms in a general's hall'.

Harlington's church still survives – with a zig-zag Norman door emblazoned with cats' heads – along with the remains of a once great yew, planted at the time of the Norman Conquest and famed for its fanciful forms.

> *'Tis strange! but She immortal grows*
> *With Age that spoils all other Beaux.*

Sadly she is old and scraggy today, but not so the renowned 'Two Peacocks' of Bedfont – giant yews that have been reclipped into their original forms of 1704. Pope wrote a satire and Thomas Hood wrote a poem on the charms of these two trees that flank the pathway leading up to the curiously quaint wooden-spired Norman church.

At Stanwell the wooden-tiled spire of St Mary's

(right) Harlington's yew

leans perilously forward, cocking an ancient snook at the airplanes taking off and landing beside it. This village has a mystifying magic today, being so close to the airport, yet with a tiny green that is surrounded by pretty-as-a-picture eighteenth- and nineteenth-century houses. Lord Knyvett's school of 1624 still stands only feet from the wire-mesh perimeter fence at one end of the village while, at the other, the ornate stone gates of his house still rear up into the sky, their stone urns almost scraping the undercarriages of Boeing 707s. They lead you into the grounds of Stanwell Place, where a great house stood from the 1000s until 1964, when the last building was demolished after the death of its occupant, King Feisal of Iraq. Henry VIII snatched the manor from the de Windsor family in 1594 and fragments of the King's stables still survive in this now derelict ground.

It is here that the final plans were made for the Normandy landings during the Second World War, and the Mulberry Harbours – those great floating ports invented by Sir John Watson Gibson, which enabled the allies to land – were actually tested on the ponds that survive to this day. Churchill, Eisenhower and Montgomery, with the Allied Command, all stood together on their banks, as the conclusive step of the war was planned.

James I's little daughter Mary died here, having been sent out of London to live with the Knyvetts in the 1600s and it was from here that Lord Knyvett sallied forth to foil the Gunpowder Plot. His monument is by Nicholas Stone, master mason to both James I and Charles I.

Apropos of gunpowder, the first to be manufactured in the British Isles was made on the flatlands of Hounslow Heath in 1346. It was then used for the

Poet IOHN SAXY upon his YEW~TREE Nov.r 1720.

Tho D'oyly of the Norman Race,
and Nobler Counts our Village grace,
Yet higher than them all Yew Tree
Derives her Stock, call'd Pedigree:
And yields to Arlington a Fame
Much Louder than it's Earldom Name:
Nor can learn'd Herauld easily tell
Whither her Arms, or Face excell.
The Conquerors Shield of Oldest Note
Veils to his Elder Taxas Coat:
His Scutcheon & whole Armour yield
To th' Bow & Arrow in her Field;
Nor was his blooming Youthfull Face
More smooth, than is her Aged Grace.
Her beauty with her years increase,
Her Shapes improve, so doth her Dress,
Deep Seams & Wrinkles once She shewd,
But these with Time are throughly cur'd.
Tis strange! but She immortal grows
With Age, that spoils all other Beaux.
Within, tis true, She's not so sound,
But Hollow from the top to ground;
But finest Ladys, we are told,
Are so, when made of London Mould.
Welcome, whether foul or Fair,
To climb up her all Comers are:
And as from Top of Monument
To View the Town, & all that's in't.
But tho too open she's at Heart,
She's close in every other part.
Her Circling Arms do strongly clasp,
Her Sprigs like Misers fingers grasp,
And Weave her Coat so Thick & Even,
Tis proof against all storms from Heaven.

Her Hoop (the Taylers Canopy)
Above her heels hangs ten foot high:
So thick, so fine, so full, so wide,
A Troop of Guards may under it Ride,
Guarded with Roundheads eight as bigg
As Jubbernole, the Giants Head;
They're lively all not one Num-skull,
Let Rome call such their Capitol.
Upon this charming Hoop doth lye
An honest stedfast Ten foot Die:
No Gamesters Box can make it rattle,
It nev'r will dance, tho' next to Fiddle:
Tis cover'd with a round green mantle,
Girt close about her, near the middle,
We call it the second Canopy,
Which over hangs the unshaken Die:
From thence mounts up a Pyramid,
A wonder first in Egypt bred:
And on its Top a ten foot Globe,
Atlas nev'r bore a finer load.
From thence springs upon highest Twigg
(As Ld Mayor made of little Prigg)
A weather Cock, who gapes to crow it
This Globe is mine, and all below it.
Masters if you approve these Lays,
And shaver Saxy deign to praise,
Crown him with Yew, instead of Bays
Be kind to Iohn your Tree who Trims
With easy Rhimes, but aching Limbs,
So, when grown Old, you too may have
your faults all mended near the grave,
And may your Resurrection be
Gay as it's Emblem, Old Yew Tree.

Revived by
WILLIAM COTTREL
Clerk 1770

Cannon at King's Arbour

Cellars at Cranford House

benches. Colnbrook

Cox's Summerhouse, Colnbrook

Gates to Stanwell Place

St Mary's

St Peters + St Pauls, Harlington

Harmondsworth

St Mary's Stanwell

St Dunstans, Cranford

Boeing 747-400

Cranford House Stables

the Green, Stanwell

'To be in Heathrow is to be in the historic bosom of the British Isles'

first time in the Battle of Crécy. In the eighteenth century there were powder mills galore in these parts which exploded with terrifying irregularity, sending vibrations as far afield as Worcestershire and Hampshire. Horace Walpole lamented that he had never seen his house at Strawberry Hill 'looking more gothic in all its born days' with 'its painted windows having all been blown out by the blast from Hounslow'.

From its early days as rough heathland – when, thanks to the wasteful habits of Londoners, Hounslow had more pigs per acre than anywhere else in the country – this area was to become the most bountiful in the British Isles. With the two-way traffic

The tomb of he who foiled the gunpowder plot

stood. In a glorious gesture both to the past and the future, 'Common Ground' – an organization founded to encourage local people to relish their surroundings – have planted an orchard of the Cox's Orange Pippin and its offspring. Benches have been designed in the shape of the letters C, O, X, and incised with the history of the apple. Richard Cox died aged seventy-nine, never knowing that his fruit would become a phenomenon. He is buried at St Mary's, Harmondsworth, another village that has retained a soothingly rural air, not forgetting the largest tithe barn in the British Isles!

Cranford has been badly ruined, slashed through by two major roads and scrunched between the airport and the M4. Hard by a roaring traffic-ridden junction of dual carriageways and motorway, there is a tiny bridge over the River Crane. It was beneath its stones that the actress Fanny Kemble 'floated by on a little skiff singing Border ballads ... entrancing the soul of Grantly Berkeley' who lived in the great house that once stood in the now-public park. According to Fanny the Berkeleys had a 'vein of singularity unlike others'. Certainly the Countess was colourful. A butcher's daughter from Gloucester, she had six sons, the first four illegitimate. Living in constant terror of arrest for perjury – having made false claims about the date of the marriage – she built an escape route through tunnels under the park for a quick getaway. Of all the survivals around Heathrow these tunnels are the most surprising: brick and vaulted like an undercroft of a church beneath an anonymous greensward. The Berkeleys' stables, too, are still standing – Dutch gabled and inset with a great clock from Hampton Court Palace – built to serve their yellow-jacketed hunt which pursued foxes as far as Charing Cross.

St Dunstan's Church, almost grazed by the M4, is rich with historical associations. Thomas Fuller,

of the fruit harvest and human fertiliser, business was booming! One of the apple growers was Richard Cox of Poyle whose little summerhouse still stands in the car park of a block of flats where his orchard once author of *The Worthies of England*, was rector here in the mid-1600s. When he died his corpse was brought to Cranford from London accompanied by three hundred 'fully robed' clergymen on horseback. A plaque to his memory is in the church, sadly not with the inscription 'Here lies Fuller's earth' as he had wanted. There are memorials of most peculiar note in the chancel, all of them lit by a 'musical' stained-glass window that was reputedly designed by Mendelssohn. One is to Charles Scarborough, the physician to Charles II and James II – who also saved Pepys's life – and the other commemorates Sir Roger Aston, portrayed life-size in brilliant colour, who was dentist and barber to James I. Elizabeth, Countess of Berkeley's monument – as delicate as Aston's is dashing – was sculpted by Nicholas Stone in Bernini's workshop in Rome. It has even been said that the great master lent his own hand.

Dr John Wilkins was rector here in 1661. Married to Oliver Cromwell's sister he was one of the first – with grim presage for the future of Heathrow – to write about life on the 'moone' and of the means of flying to it, even going so far as to construct an alarming 'land sailing carriage' in which he careered around Hounslow Heath.

An account was written of a church service at St Dunstan's in the nineteenth century when the barrel organ 'could only plead guilty to the violation of three separate tunes'. This startling instrument was operated by the village headmistress, who vigorously turned the handle, the signal to commence being a lusty blast upon a whistle blown by Mr Hickes: 'Thus, when the parson piped, the organ and the choir, more or less concurrently, began, and the three tunes had to serve alike for Psalms or for the few hymns then in customary use, without the slightest regard for meter or length of line.'

Those were the days, when the area was 'the perfection of rural repose and beauty'. As the Revd Wetenhall Wilkes was to write in his poem 'Hounslow Heath',

Hail happy scene secure from factious noise,
From pomp, from cares, from all delusive joys…
Where soaring larks awake the dewy plains,
And tempt the Muse to sing the rural scenes…
Assist, ye sacred Nine, the sports rehearse
Of HOUNSLOW HEATH – a word not seen in verse;
HOUNSLOW – unknown to all the tuneful throng,
A place ne'er mentioned in descriptive song;
Shall ancient HOUNSLOW then be lost to fame,
And dull oblivion desecrate the name?
No – from the Nine we this advice receive
That in their records HOUNSLOW's name shall live.

THIS TABLET WAS AFFIXED IN 1926 TO COMMEMORATE THE 200TH ANNIVERSARY OF THE BIRTH OF MAJOR GENERAL WILLIAM ROY, F.R.S. BORN 4TH MAY 1726 — DIED 1ST JULY 1790. HE CONCEIVED THE IDEA OF CARRYING OUT THE TRIANGULATION OF THIS COUNTRY AND OF CONSTRUCTING A COMPLETE AND ACCURATE MAP AND THEREBY LAID THE FOUNDATION OF THE ORDNANCE SURVEY THIS GUN MARKS THE N.W. TERMINAL OF THE BASE WHICH WAS MEASURED IN 1784 UNDER THE SUPERVISION OF GENERAL ROY, AS PART OF THE OPERATIONS FOR DETERMINING THE RELATIVE POSITIONS OF THE GREENWICH AND PARIS OBSERVATORIES. THIS MEASUREMENT WAS RENDERED POSSIBLE BY THE MUNIFICENCE OF H.M. KING GEORGE III WHO INSPECTED THE WORK ON 21ST AUGUST 1784. THE BASE WAS MEASURED AGAIN IN 1791 BY CAPTAIN MUDGE AS THE COMMENCEMENT OF THE PRINCIPAL TRIANGULATION OF GREAT BRITAIN LENGTH OF BASE REDUCED TO M.S.L.

And so it should.

ISLE OF BUTE

EFORE you set foot on the Island of Bute, the delights of Wemyss Bay Railway Station tune up your architectural taste buds to the treats that lie ahead. Surrounded by the cosy charms of an Edwardian railway station, you are suddenly swept along, beneath a great curvaceous cast-iron canopy, to the shores of the Firth of Clyde. There a Caledonian McBrayne ferry will bear you off to Bute – fifteen and a half miles long and three and a half miles wide – on which is to be found one of the most exotic private palaces in the British Isles. It is Mount Stuart, the fantastical pink sandstone pile that was built by the 3rd Marquess of Bute, between 1879 and 1900 when he died aged only fifty, leaving the house unfinished. In 1988 all the work that had so dramatically stopped was started up again by his great-grandson John, the 6th Marquess and his wife, Jennifer, who applied every bit as much vim and verve and lavish love for the place as did the house's creator.

For the second time the dreams for this house have been dashed by death since, with horribly sad coincidence, John Bute has died young, like his great-grandfather before him, and both of them left their remarkable schemes for Mount Stuart unrealized. They were bold and grand dreams of the kind normally associated with the nineteenth century, but here at Mount Stuart they were being given dazzling twentieth-century reality. The house is now open to the public.

It is a staggeringly strange and seemingly southern European palace – in French, Venetian and Spanish Gothic – that has been set down on a small island in Scotland. As was said when it was built: 'No structure could be less in harmony with "the Highland Hills that lie like sleeping Kings".' Mount Stuart never fails to startle. With its bizarre array of architectural protuberances as well as its grandeur and its opulence of oddity and incongruity, it is like coming upon a doge's palace in a desert or the Palace of Westminster rising out of a plain!

The house underwent a complete transmogrification; in 1840 Mount Stuart was described as having an 'external aspect like that of a dilapidated barrack, greatly requiring a few touches of the trowel from some skilful architect, to metamorphose the very plain front into a more tasteful exterior'. Thanks to a devastating fire, such advice was taken with glimmering gilded knobs on and the house was rebuilt, primed with a passion for architecture on a grand scale by the 3rd Marquess of Bute – 'The Noble Patron of the Noble Art of Architecture'.

There are few figures as convolutedly colourful in the annals of architecture: a raging romantic yet a dogged scholar, the Marquess was also responsible –

Lord Bute, 'whose hands were never out of the mortar tub'

along with the architect William Burges – for the extraordinary embellishments at Cardiff Castle and Castel Coch in Wales which have the most elaborate decoration in Britain. Nor was that all; he is also remembered for the restoration or rebuilding of some sixty other buildings. According to his architect at Mount Stuart, Rowland Anderson, 'Lord Bute's hands were never out of the mortar tub!'

Having been born the richest baby in the British Isles – with a fortune made from Cardiff's coal and docklands – he reputedly died the richest man and no halfpenny of the inheritance was ill-spent.

Lord Bute, ever serious and scholarly, had a mind that was steeped in history. He was a Catholic convert – causing a sensation in Scotland – and a deep-thinking theologian and liturgist as well as a herald and a passionate advocate of psychical research. He was an ardent medievalist and mystic as well as astrologer and archaeologist, a philanthropist and a philologist who triumphed as a linguist – mastering twenty-one tongues, including Arabic, Coptic, Chaldee and Greek. He learnt Hebrew so as to translate the entire Roman Breviary – 'to reflect the ideas of Latin in the best English mirror I could command'. Calling it 'his beloved child', it took him nine years to finish.

Above all, though, his passion was building and this he did with bravado. Mount Stuart is steeped in the scholarship and symbolism of his studies, with a great hall – sixty square feet of solid splendour – with walls and pillars of rarest marble and alabaster, all rushing up to a vaulted ceiling, emblazoned with the constellations and with mirrored stars glimmering amongst figures of the zodiac. The brilliant hues of the stained-glass windows are splashed throughout with their zodiacal and mythological forms all charging round amid swirling waves of purple, scarlet, blue and green.

Mount Stuart was built at a luxuriously leisured pace and with luxuriously liberal funds. When building this hall, Lord Bute had been very taxed as to whether to have all its pillars made in marble or granite. 'I am told', he said, 'that granite would cost £20,000 more than marble, but that is not the point. The question is which will look best.'

Throughout the house there is endearing proof of its builder's great love for animals. When a little boy he would perform an elaborate religious ceremony over any tiny corpse he came upon, and years later had scores of wallabies in the woods at Mount Stuart. He loathed shooting and a description of his attempt

The hall – sixty square feet of sheer solid splendour

at the sport was left by Sir Herbert Maxwell: 'I retain an impression of him shivering in a woodland ride, the ground being covered with snow. He had on his feet a pair of patent leather shoes and under his arm a gun which he knew not how to handle.' It is therefore no surprise to find some hundreds of creatures – marble caterpillars and butterflies, snails and snakes – occupying honoured and permanent havens among the marble flowers of the house.

The carving on the pillar capitals at Mount Stuart give the clearest clues to the history of the house. Where one might bulge with the beauty of a bird amongst raspberries (carved in such deep relief that you can get your fingers behind all the leaves and stalks), the next will be a bulbous blank. This would be a spot where, on the death of the 3rd Marquess, some sixty workmen had all stopped in their tracks – after twenty-one painstaking years – with the house still unfinished. In 1988 those tools were taken up again, when John and Jennifer Bute commissioned a galaxy of craftsmen, not only to finish the work of 1900 but also to make grand declarations of their own. Francesca Pelizzoli's muscular murals of the early 1990s live happily under the same roof as the Gothic swimming pool of the 1890s and Tom Errington's painted ceilings – either started from scratch or finished from where the 3rd Marquess left off – dazzlingly proclaim their modernity whilst harmonizing with their surroundings.

John Bute – the twentieth-century Prince among Patrons of the Arts in Scotland – was my hero and my friend whom I loved and admired with all my heart. His sights were set high for Mount Stuart, soaring, for example, up to the clerestory of his great white chapel – forever red from the blood-coloured glass – for which he was commissioning the painting and carving of a multitude of saints and angels. With his passion for the arts and crafts, no one could have been better suited to take on the task of finishing the house. Whereas most would have sunk on inheriting such a palace, he not only swam but relished the course of restoring, conserving and recreating his great-grandfather's dream. I will never forget the sight of his mother engulfed by yards of plans for putting back giant tiled women on either side of the drawing room fireplace. It was she who had ripped them out years before. She also lived to see the renewed glory of a great Gothic arch over the same fireplace – an arch that years earlier she had made the entrance to the vegetable garden.

Because of his early death John Bute never entirely fulfilled his dream, but what he did was magnificent. When he died an obituarist wrote that 'The Almighty will surely have already put him in guardianship of his many mansions in heaven in acknowledgement of his diligence thereto on earth … our final salute at his departure will be drowned by the fanfare that will greet him in Heaven.'

A marble spider amid marble tulips

Sir John's Museum

AMID the chaste charms of a London square, you suddenly come upon it – what in its day was described as 'a very odd shell – denoting the abode of a very odd fish'. It is the house, museum and library of the architect Sir John Soane at Lincoln's Inn Fields in London.

Soane stands alone in having created an architectural style, as well as a house of such bizarre beauty that it continues to baffle every bit as much today as it did when it was created boldly two hundred years ago. By reinvigorating and reinventing the classical architecture of the past, Soane created forms that were entirely his own. His house is the very paragon of those peculiarities. It gives a shock as you turn each corner, having no notion what the next trick or treat might be. There can be no other building of such curious contradictions as this: so clear yet convoluted; its sheer classical lines wrought into a cat's cradle of complexities. They soar up and they swoop down; they stop, they start; they change levels and they shoot off in all directions. Vistas are elongated and terminated – enclosing and disclosing, concealing and revealing and never failing to surprise with their combination of convention and spectacular lack of conformity. And, as if this were not enough, these effects are often multiplied tenfold by mirrors unex-

pectedly built into walls, on pillars and around ceilings. Despite these and a thousand other surprises Soane's is a style that has reduced classicism to its quintessential elements.

Numbers 12, 13 and 14 Lincoln's Inn Fields – three houses were built into one – were designed as his house and museum between 1782 and 1797 while critics clamoured their displeasure. 'No exertions should be spared to check the adoption of his manner,' fulminated one. 'It is of the most pernicious and vitiated. Nature, common sense, propriety, simplicity, are all immolated to his idol, Novelty. He has not the slightest conception of the chaste, the grand, or the sublime of his art. There is nothing wanting but frequent violations of propriety.' Soane was even taken to court for 'contravening the building act' with his dastardly design. The case had been brought by William Kennard, an 'impudent' surveyor, described as 'fat, and fierce in consequence of being adorned with a magnificent pair of mustachios!' Counter critics rose up in defence of the building, such as Robert Burdon who wrote to his friend: 'I have had more than once a strong desire to have a peep at your "castle" at Linc's Inn Fields, both for the sake of saying how d'ye do to its inhabitants, and also to see what extraordinary outworks you have fortified yourself, so as to provide the attacks of the angry surveyor. I was glad to see however that you have defended Yourself and your castle strenuously and successfully. You have, in martial language, "covered yourself with Glory".'

Then there was Peter Cole who penned a poem to the great architect in 1832:

> *Soane! in thy character is found combined,*
> *All that a bard could wish to grace his lays!*
> *Bounty and skill that mark superior mind,*
> *And gain a nation's gratitude and praise.*
> *Soane! The important task was thine,*
> *With all thy thirst for classic lore,*
> *To take thine own distinctive line*
> *And forms create unknown before.*

We can judge for ourselves, as the house in Lincoln's Inn Fields is exactly as he left it, with every object where he placed it – all his idiosyncratic arrangements protected in perpetuity by the Soane Museum Act of Parliament – a private bill he had passed in 1833 for the benefit of 'Amateurs and Students of Painting, Sculpture and Architecture'. He lived in Lincoln's Inn between 1792 and 1837, honing his home into 'A Temple of Art', obsessively furnishing and filling, rebuilding and extending, 'distending its little body to the upmost endurance of its skin'. It was built as a monument to inspire and instruct through the magic of architecture, which for him was always 'Queen of the Fine Arts' ('with painting and sculpture her handmaidens').

The strangeness of his genius embraces you as soon as you step inside the door. The Breakfast Room is the first surprise. It is a square room with an oblong canopy-like dome supported by mirrored columns and, on either side of the ceiling, gaps have been left through which light pours in a most unexpected way. Strangest of all is the feeling of freshness that pervades these forms. Soane's is a style that seems to

positively sing of today. He wrote of the room in 1835: 'The views ... into the Monument Court and ... the Museum, the mirrors in the ceiling, and the looking glass, combined with the variety of outline and general arrangement in the design and decoration of this limited space, present a succession of those fanciful effects which constitute the poetry of Architecture.'

And so it is with the whole house and its endlessly curious series of spaces – like some beautiful yet crazed jigsaw made complete by having missing pieces. The oldest and most spectacular part of the museum is 'The Dome' – a space rising up the full height of the building that is brimful of plaster casts as well as stone and marble carvings of antiquity. Soane had acquired such rarities as a marble 'capital of a pilaster from the interior of the Pantheon at Rome', as well as a fragment of a female figure from the Acropolis in Athens and his treasures are chock-a-block throughout the house. A bust of the great man himself stands sentinel over his acquisitions under the Dome. It was sculpted by his friend Sir Francis Chantrey in 1827. 'Will you come with me on Thursday morning,' wrote Sir Francis for the first sitting, 'and bring your head with you.' Soane was described as distinguished-looking, 'taller than was common' and so thin as to appear taller still. A fellow architect, George Wightwick, said that he looked like a reflection on the back of a spoon! His bust faces the cast of Apollo Belvedere – made for Lord Burlington – and for which Soane 'set so much value' that he had to take down 'a large portion of the external wall in order to admit it to its present position'. Beyond the Dome, the Colonnade creates yet another singular space topped up with treasures, such as the 4 BC

(right) 'Like some beautiful but crazed jigsaw'

Dea Multimamma, the many-breasted goddess

Greek sepulchral reliefs, a Roman table leg and an occult marble statue of the Ephesian Diana – otherwise known as the Dea Multimamma, the many-breasted goddess.

You are led into a corridor ablaze with golden light – one of the many areas designed by Soane so as to give Mediterranean life to his vast collection of antiquities. By bathing them in their rightful sun of the south, he saw to it that his treasures would be seen to their greatest advantage – always imploring visitors not to come in 'dirty weather'. Seen from above, the roof of the museum is an architectural hedgehog of yellow glazed protuberances; with barrel vaults, as well as gables and truncated pyramids, all sticking up into the sky.

The studious heart of the house, the drawing office – again hung heavy with marble fragments and casts from antiquity – can be glimpsed from the Dome, its window cut into the wall on high 'affording a bird's eye view … of the museum'. From his first day in Lincoln's Inn Soane had employed pupils, who would come aged fifteen or sixteen to work for twelve hours a day – Monday to Saturday – for five years. Here they could learn the orders of architecture surrounded by the real thing, or a cast of the real thing, immediately to hand. It was like working within a living pattern book, that showed everything that they needed to know of ancient Greece and Rome but, of course, could never afford to see. The students kept company, too, with one object of curious rather than classical distinction: a 'glazed case containing the Mummies of two Cats, one found in Lothbury … between the wall and wainscoting of a Room, with a rat in its mouth and the other in Lord Yarboro's house in Chelsea'.

Soane, with his 'impressive dignity and flashing eyes' (according to Wightwick) was the grand master presiding over all. Intoning in Biblical language when moved, his voice would curiously rise and fall – 'up towards a squeak, or down to a mild guttural'. The more 'teeming his wrath' the more 'diminishing' his tone; 'fury in its last excess, was signified by a terrific silence!' The young architect Robert Smirke wrote of the worries when working for Soane: 'He was on Monday morning in one of his "amiable" Tempers. Everything was slovenly that I was doing. My

Pages from a giant's book – the picture gallery transformed

drawing was slovenly because it was too great a scale, my scale also … was excessively "slovenly", and that I should draw it out again on the back, not to waste another sheet.' It was said that Sir John had 'the nerves of a cat'. Wightwick went so far as to say that he 'had never seen anyone out of a lunatic asylum so bereft of reason's influence'.

In 1824, when he was seventy-one years old, Soane built the Picture Room which, with the creation of hinged walls that move and multiply, is quite simply the work of a wizard. The sight of Hogarth's *Rake's Progress and An Election* is exciting enough, but little prepares you for Soane's supreme surprise when, with the merest movement, the walls – like pages in a giant's book – swing gently forward in your hands. Appearing apparition-like from within themselves they transform a modest room of 12 feet by 13 feet into a great picture gallery, which, if measured for its hanging space, would be 20 feet wide and 40 feet long!

To one side of the room, drawings by Piranesi are concealed behind the hinged walls, while on the other there are the glorious works of Joseph Gandy – the architect and draughtsman 'of the first order' who delicately transposed Soane's schemes to paper. His watercolour, *Architectural Visions of Early Fancy and Dreams in the Evening of Life*, shows a dream vision of Soane's earliest plans, including the staggering Triumphal Bridge of 1776, for which Soane won the Royal Academy Gold Medal – aged only twenty-three – which was to be the momentous start of his idiosyncratic career. Painted atop this mirage of a mountain is one of his proposals for a mausoleum with space for eighty-four coffins and twenty-four funerary urns. Soane had designed such an outlandish memorial in 1777 for his student friend, James King, who had drowned the year before. Wending its way through the architectural dreamscape is Lord Nelson's funeral procession, ostrich feathers flying on the ornate hearse as it passes beneath one of the two arches designed in 1796 as 'entrances from Piccadilly into the Royal Parks'. Sadly, his magnificent design for 'A Residence for a Canine Family in Ancient Times' was not thought worthy of such august company, nor were his classical nesting boxes or his remarkable cowshed, bedecked with a dome, arched entrances, urns, obelisks and a life-size stone cow!

After the magic of his 'Movable Planes', as Soane called them, there is yet another surprise in store when you pull the last wall aside, only to find yourself facing yet another vision of statuary and stained glass, as well as architectural models and drawings, all of them unbelievably suspended over a deep and dark abyss of Gothic gloom. Soane had always disliked this style, writing that he 'should as soon think of going back to the primitive hut, or the wigwam for the Indians as to the Gothic'. He railed against the rise of the Gothic revival, scornful of its barbarism in secular use and mocking this 'Modern' movement for becoming the 'New National Architecture' of the land. As a picturesque shock though, in these chastely classical surroundings, no surprise could be greater than the Gothic and to satirize the style, his 'Monk's Parlour' was born – filled with grotesques (many from the old House of Lords) and shrouded in gloom. He even created the ruins of a monastery to add to the sombreness of the scene. A soaring stone monument built to mark the remains of 'Padre Giovanni' in fact was to become the outsize memorial to Mrs Soane's tiny dog, Fanny, who had outlived her mistress by five years. The little creature had become Soane's faithful companion, 'the delight, the solace of his leisure hours'. She died on Christmas Day in 1820. 'Alas poor Fanny,' lamented Soane, 'faithful, affectionate, disinterested friend. Farewell.' James Ward painted the dog's portrait in 1822, showing her appealing

elegantly to her master amid the classical columns of ancient Greece.

One of the rarest of all Soane's possessions, and certainly the most costly, was the alabaster cover for the Egyptian Pharaoh Seti I's sarcophagus of 1300 BC from the necropolis at Thebes. Carved by the worshippers of Osiris with as yet undecipherable hieroglyphics, it had been discovered in 1821 by Giovanni Belzoni, the giant strongman, engineer and explorer. Soane had bought the sarcophagus for £2000 and held three 'grand receptions' by lamplight for 'distinguished fashionables and literary characters … private friends and elegant females' to view his treasure. The diarist and painter Benjamin Robert Haydon wrote of being there: 'The first person I met … was Coleridge … I was pushed against Turner, the landscape painter with his red face and white waistcoat, and … was carried off my legs and irretrievably bustled to where the sarcophagus lay. Soane's house is a perfect labyrinth … It was the finest fun imaginable to see the people come into the Library after wandering about below, amidst tombs and capitals, and shafts, and noseless heads, with a sort of expression of delighted relief at finding themselves again among the living, and with coffee and cake. Fancy delicate ladies of fashion dipping their pretty heads into an old mouldy, fusty, hierogloiphicked coffin,

'Faithful, affectionate, disinterested friend'

blessing their stars at its age, wondering whom it contained and whispering that it was mentioned in Pliny … Just as I was beginning to meditate, the Duke of Sussex, with a star on his breast and asthma inside it, came squeezing and wheezing along the narrow passage, driving all the women before him like a Blue-Beard, and putting his royal head into the coffin added his wonder to the wonder of the rest.' The house was alive with light; with 'Glass Bucket Lamps' and 'Glass Barrell Lamps' and with one hundred and eight other chandeliers, candelabras, lamps and candles – illuminating the entire building save for the 'Cript' down deep in the basement, where the white translucent alabaster sarcophagus shone forth alone in the dark.

Soane's friend Mrs Hofland was there: 'Had any one of the gay company,' she wrote, 'been placed ALONE in the Sepulchral chamber at the "witching hour of night" when the flickering lights became self-extinguished and the last murmuring sounds without, ceased to speak of the living world – it is probable that even the healthiest pulse would have been affected by the darker train of emotions which a situation so unallied to common life is calculated to produce. The awe ameliorated by beauty and softened by tender reminiscences would be exchanged for the myst-erious expectation of some terrific visitant from the invisible world.'

Oh, would that the 'terrific visitant' could be the great Soane himself. He once wrote, 'The architect should think, and feel as a Poet, combine and em-bellish as a Painter, and execute as a Sculptor.' How we should congratulate him for practising so perfectly what he preached.

Fanny – Soane's faithful companion

KENSAL GREEN

OOK north from the elevated A40 at Shepherd's Bush in London and you will see an immense swathe of countryside cutting through the chimneys. By day it is green and by night, jet black. It is the General Cemetery of All Souls, Kensal Green – in 1833 the first cemetery to be built in the capital. Behind a high wall and entered through a white Doric gateway, there must surely be a perpetual party going on. For, if there is life after death, you could find no more interesting assembly of characters to relish their surroundings than those who are gathered together here.

This glittering company of nineteenth-century luminaries are forever celebrated with buildings and memorial sculpture of every conceivable architectural style. The whole gamut of nineteenth-century life is there: from Charles Wingfield who invented lawn tennis, to Wilkie Collins, author of *The Woman in White*, while Isambard Kingdom Brunel lies beneath a granite block within earshot of his Great Western Railway. Decimus Burton who designed the Palm House at Kew is buried here, and so is Philip Hardwick, architect of the Euston Arch. John Chatterton, harpist to Queen Victoria, flies the musical flag, as does Charles Coote, the Duke of Devonshire's private pianist who was in constant musical attendance for over thirty years. The most unlikely musician of all though is George Polgreen Bridgtower, a mulatto violinist to whom the 'Kreutzer' Sonata was originally dedicated. After a quarrel 'about a girl' Beethoven had 'scratched' out Bridgtower's name and replaced it with Kreutzer's – whom he had never met. Brischdauer, as Beethoven called him, lies within the same cemetery walls as Sir Charles Locock, who delivered all Queen Victoria's children. Their nurse, Mrs Thurston, is buried here too – all of them cast by fate to be neighbours for eternity.

To visit Kensal Green is to explore the highways and byways of Victorian life, to plunge into the culture of the times. For example, there is Sir Richard Mayne, the founder of the Metropolitan Police, whose great granite obelisk is only feet away from the memorial to Frederick Winsor, who brought gas lighting to the capital's hitherto dark streets. This was 'offensive, dangerous, expensive and unmanageable', wrote Walter Scott, 'he must be a madman who proposed to light the streets of London with smoke'. His epitaph is blasphemous but most illuminating: 'I am come a light into the world that whosoever believe in me should not abide in darkness'.

As in life, so too in death, here at Kensal Green it is a small world, with many of its inhabitants having known, or been connected to, one another in all manner of ways. William Makepeace Thackeray, for example, is separated by only one grave from his Charterhouse schoolfriend John Leech, the cartoonist. They not only grew up together, but were given their first jobs at the same time by the editor of *Punch*, Charles Shirley Brooks – who himself lies but a leap away. According to the *Kensal Green Handbook*, Thackeray's funeral was 'modest' with Dickens as one of the chief mourners, along with Browning and the painters Millais and Frith. There were occasional melancholy interruptions of weeping but 'more obtrusive were the cracks of the sportsmen's rifles from the neighbouring fields, causing the horses to champ their bits in noisy restlessness'. It must have been a huge coffin as Thackeray was over six foot three inches tall and his head housed a brain weighing fifty-eight and a half ounces: 'One of the greatest brains that England ever knew … its fiery fervour, its superb indignation against hypocrisy, pretension and deceit … is now hushed in the terrible serenity of death.' John Leech was also at the funeral – only a year before he was to take up permanent residence at Kensal Green – and Anthony Trollope, also at the graveside, would be buried in the cemetery nineteen years later.

It was Trollope, of course, who introduced the letter box to the British Isles and Kensal Green is populous with his fellow postal reformers. Thomas

John Leech's caricature of Mulready's design for the first penny postage envelope

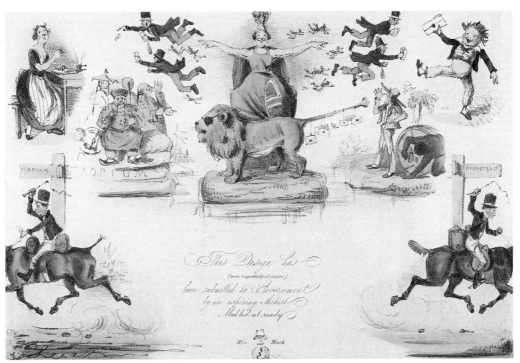

and Warren de la Rue – beneath a gothic domed plinth – invented the first envelope folding machine as well as printed postage stamps. Then there is William Mulready, the artist who designed the first pre-paid envelope. He is commemorated in Central Avenue – the apple of Kensal Green's architectural eye – by a magnificent Renaissance-style canopied tomb, under which he lies on a fringed and wonderfully woven straw mat of artificial stone. The tools of his trade are carved around the base with representations of his paintings in bas-relief. Francis Freeling, who masterminded the early days of the post office and who organized the first free deliveries to the home, is buried within whispering distance. His monument, now a curiously squat column, was originally five times taller and it stands a few feet away from the sadly depleted memorial – minus a bronze bust – of his greatest friend, Thomas Hood, the poet. So firm indeed was their friendship that Hood christened his daughter 'Francis Freeling' – surname and all. Her father had a sad life. Racked by consumption and wrecked by debt, he was said to have mortgaged his brain for money from his publishers.

Another of Hood's friends, John Liston, the comedian, lies nearby: 'all that is left of that quaint genius', lamented a visitor in 1880, 'that we were wont to laugh at so boisterously'. The critic Hazlitt wrote, 'his face is bathed with jests!' Roars of applause therefore must be echoing around Kensal Green, with so many of his friends hard at hand, including the actor Charles Kemble and his daughter Fanny.

And so it goes on, the tapestry of life woven into a web of death. Inventors and pioneers such as Edward Cator Seaton, who was responsible for compulsory vaccination, lie side by side with entertainers like Andrew Ducrow who is buried beneath an outlandish Graeco-Egyptian mausoleum. This is 'ponderous coxcombery', growled *The Builder* in 1836 on seeing the monument that was built to honour Ducrow's wife and eventually himself. Dreadful scenes took place at Mrs Ducrow's burial when her husband, on seeing that the ground was still full of water, shouted at the priest that he was 'a swindling old humbug' and marched off with the cemetery keys. A flamboyant showman, Ducrow was famed for the peculiarly picturesque *Poses Plastiques Equestres*, in which he struck attitudes as Zephyr, Mercury or a 'Yorkshire Foxhunter' whilst riding or driving as many as nine horses for the display. The creatures were 'but the air on which he flew', wrote one enraptured critic: 'what Godlike grace in that volant motion, fresh from Olympus, ere new lighted on some Heaven kissing hill'. There were elegant variations, with Ducrow – in skin-tight marbled attire – motionless upon a plinth. He would then gradually change from one antique statue into another. 'Raphael's Dream' was particularly popular. He died within a few days of his favourite horse, John Lump, in 1842. The hat and gloves he wore as Charles II lie on a broken column beside the mausoleum – all in stone.

With such architectural extravaganzas as this, in a landscape of classical temples, columns, canopies and obelisks as well as Gothic arches, spires and pinnacles, the cemetery is a dream-like amalgam of architectural forms. Although 'The Battle of the Styles' was raging when the cemetery was built, the final result for Kensal Green was one of happy contrast rather than conflict.

With a heritage like this, how can funerary art have sunk to its present dire and devastating depths? The improvements that have swept through the architectural world have by-passed this miniature branch of structural design. Visiting the cemeteries and graveyards of today is like being in the saddest development of the 1960s but with one hideous difference: that they are still being built hand over fist with the

Andrew Ducrow – 'What Godlike grace in that volant motion'

same blinkered fervour of the post-war years. Great tracts of consecrated land have fallen victim to what can only be described as a grotesque modernistic world in miniature. Rules and regulations as to the size, height and material of memorials have resulted in the grimmest uniformity. Democracy in life has become dictatorship in death, with every one of us forced to suffer a Ceauçescu-like regiment of marble and stone blocks marching roughshod over our remains. Even the most architecturally aware now have to end their days under a blighting block on the landscape. The cemeteries of the past were intended as morally uplifting oases, reflecting the ideals of the age. What in Heaven's name is represented by the sterile stumps of today – relieved only by grisly green marble chippings? There is one lone beacon of hope: 'Memorials by Artists' run by Harriet Frazer in Suffolk, who will put you in touch with craftsmen, and then fight the what should be unnecessary battles with the Diocesan boards. Slowly but surely a new and vibrant crop of funereal sculpture is starting to appear in churchyards and cemeteries throughout Britain. As yet this is not to be at Kensal Green where contemporary stones still stand harshly stark in these Elysian fields.

'What in Heaven's name is represented by the sterile stumps of today'

Eric Gill designed a memorial for Marigold Churchill, the two-and-a-half-year-old daughter of Winston and Clementine who died of meningitis in 1921. Sadly it was vandalized and a stone cross with children at its base was stolen. In the 1970s it was replaced by a simpler version by her surviving sister, Mary Soames. Eric Gill's inscription still survives. Marigold, who was born four days after Armistice Day in 1918, had always been known as Duckadilly. A year after her death Churchill's grief was still raw when he wrote to his wife: 'I pass through again those sad scenes last year, when we lost our dear Duckadilly. Poor lamb, it is a gaping wound whenever one

Wm Harrison Ainsworth (1805-82) Novelist. * Lady Laura Theresa Alma Tadema (1852-1909) - M. Sir Lawrence Alma Tadema.* Chas Babbage (1792-1871) - Father of the computer, his brain at the R Coll of Surgeons) * Michl Wm Balfe (1808-79) - Composer * Thomas Barnes (1785-1841) the 'thunderer' ed. of The Times * James Barry (1796-1865) - woman disguised as man. Army Surgeon * Sir William Beatty (d.1842) - Lord Nelson's Surgeon at Trafalgar *Sir Julius Benedict (1794-1885) - Composer 'Lilly of Killarney' *Geo Birkbeck (1776-1841) - Founder Birkbeck College *Emile Blondin (1824-97) - Tightrope Walker * Richd Vicars Boyle (1822-1908) - Indian Mutiny Hero, laid out Japanese Railways * George Polgreen Bridgtower (1778-1860) - Mulatto violinist to whom Beethoven originally dedicated Kreutzer Sonata * Dr Richd Bright (1789-1858) Surgeon to Queen Victoria. Dis.Bright's Disease * Charles William Shirley Brooks (1816-74) - Editor 'Punch' * Isambard Kingdom Brunel (1806-69) - Engr.G.W.R. * Sir Marc Isambard BRUNEL (1769-1849) - Engr.Thames Tunnel * Wm Burn (1789-1870) - Archt, Fonthill * Decimus Burton (1800-81) - Archt, Palm House Kew * Lady Isabella Noel Byron (1792-1860) -m. Lord Byron *John Caradoc (1799-1873) - A.D.C. to Wellington. Ambassador Brazil & Spain * George Carden - Founder of Kensal Green Cemetery * Sir Ernest Cassel (1852-1921) - Creator of Moroccan,Turkish & Egyptian Banks, buried in gold & silver coffin * John Cassell (1817-65) - Founder Publisher * John Balsir Chatterton (1802-71) - Harpist to Queen Victoria * Marigold Frances Churchill (1918-1922) - Daughter of Sir Winston * Sir Caspar Purden Clarke (1846-1911) - Dir. V&A & Metropolitan Museum of Art New York * Henry Robert Clifton (1832-72) - 'Handsome Harry' Music Hall Singer* Sir Alexander James Edward Cockburn (1792-1880) - Judge Titchborne Claimant Trial * Sir Geo Cockburn (1772-1853) - Admiral, conveyed Napoleon to St Helena * Wm Wilkie Collins (1824-89) Writer.The Woman in White * Chas Coote (1809-90) - Private pianist to Duke of Devonshire * Sir Michael Costa (1810-84) - Composer. 1st to conduct with baton in England * Sir Joseph Arthur Crowe (1825-96) Crimean Correspondent Ill. London News. Indian Mutiny Correspondent The Times. * Geo Cruikshank (1792-1878) - Cartoonist (Memorial only) * Thos Daniell (1749-1840) - Painter of India * John Constantine De COURCY (1827-65) Last to Practice 'De Courcy Privilege' of keeping hat on with Royalty * Sir Henry Thomas De La Beche (1796-1855) - Founder Nat'l Geographic Survey *Thos De La Rue (1793-1866)- inventor of 1st printed playing card * Gen Sir Collingham Dickson V.C. (1817-1904) Siege of Sebastapol * Sir Chas Wentworth Dilke (1843-1911) - Statesman destroyed by scandal * Chas Wentworth Dilke (1789-1864) - Critic * Andrew Ducrow (1793-1842) - Equestrian Showman * Jas Dunlop - Pneumatic tyre manufacturer * Joseph Durham (1814-1877) - Sculptor * Sir Chas Lock Eastlake (1793-1865) - Artist * Chas Lock Eastlake (1836-1906) - Archt Artist Writer *John Passmore Edwards (1823-1911) - Philanthropist * Dr John Elliotson (1791-1868) - Physician. 1st to use stethoscope * Giovanni Baptista Falcieri (d.1874) Byron's Manservant * Hugh Falconer (1808-65) - Superintendent Botanical Gardens, Calcutta * Alleyn Fitzherbert. Lord St Helens (1753-1839) Amb.to Russia, Lord of Bedchamber to George III * Richd Flexmore (1824-60) - Clown, 'A fellow of infinite jest' * John Forster (1812-76) - Historian Biographer * Angelica Patience Frazer (1823-1910) - 'The Tailor's Friend' Philanthropist * Sir Francis Freeling (1764-1836) - Postal reformer.* Wm Powell FRITH (1819-1909) - Artist 'Derby Day' & 'Railway Station' * John Gibson (1817-92) - Architect * Geo Wm Charles, Duke Of Cambridge (1819-1904) Grandson of George III C in C Army Buried With 'Wife' Sarah Fairbrother, Pantomine actress & their three sons * Sir John Goss (1800-80) Composer.Wellington's Funeral Anthem * Sir Hugh Henry Gough V.C.(1833-1909) -Indian Mutiny * Tho Handcock (1786-1865) - Inventor vulcanised rubber. *Phillip Hardwick (1792-1870) - Archt, Euston Arch. * John Harley Pritt (1786-1858) - Counter Tenor known as 'Fat Jack' for his thinness * Sir Henry Hawkins (1817-1903) - Prosecuting Counsel Titchborne Claimant Trial Sophia Hawthorne (D.1871) Artist.Writer.m. Nathaniel Hawthorne * Sir Geo Head (1782-1858) - Dep Marshall at William IV's & Queen Victoria's Coronations * Henry Heatherington (1792-1849) - His writings inspired Chartist Movement * John Cam Hobhouse (1786-1869) - Whig Minister. Writer, Byron's Best Man * May Scott Hogarth (1819-37) Apple Of Dickens' Eye.* Lady Saba Holland (d.1866) - Writer Daughter of Rev Sidney Smith m. Sir Henry Holland * Baron Gunther Von Holzhausen (1882-1905) - Shot himself for love of Music Hall Artiste Gertie Miller in her boudoir * Thos Hood (1799-1845) - Poet * John Calcott Horsley (1817-1903) - R.A.Executed decoration in House of Lords. * John Pryke Hullah (1812-84) - Composer.Inv of System to teach as many as 50,000 musicians at same time * James Henry Leigh Hunt (1784-1859) Editor, Essayist & Critic,1st to acclaim both Keats & Shelly * Cecilia Letitia Duchess Of Inverness (d.1873) - Duke of Sussex's 'Wife' * Owen Jones (1809-74) - Archt, Superintendent Gt Exhibition * Charles Kemble (d.1864) - Actor * Fanny Kemble (1809-93) - Actress * Imre Kiralfy (1845-1919) -Writer. Des White City Stadium (Memorial only) * Sir Wm Knighton (1776-1826) - Physician & Keeper of Privy Purse to George IV * Sarah Lane (1822-99) - Actress 'The Pantomine Fairy she played at Christmas was less important than the everyday fairy she played among the homes of the poor' * Wm Leftwich (1770-1843) Pioneer in refrigeration * John Leech (1817-64) - Cartoonist * John Liston (1776-1865) - Comedian * Jos Locke (1805-60) - Engr * Charlotte Sophia Lockhart (1799-1837) d of Sir Walter Scott .

Sir Chas Locock (1799-1875) - Queen Victoria's 'Accoucheur' delivered all her children *John St John Long (1798-1834) - Quack Doctor * John Claudius Loudon (1783-1843) - Landscape Gardener. Archt, Writer * Wm Edward Love (1797-1868) - imitator of every sound under the sun * Sir Wm Lumley (1769-1850) - Gov.of Bermuda, faked episcopal powers, Queen Victoria's Groom of Bedchamber * Sir Jas McGrigor (1771-1858) - Chief of Medical Staff in Peninsular Army *Chas McKay (1814-89) - Ed.Illustrated London News. Times reporter on American Civil War,.wrote 'The Good Times Coming' * Donald MacKay (d.1894) - Piper to Prince of Wales * Donald Maclise (1806-70) - Historian & Shakespearean Painter * Wm Chas MacReady (1793-1873) - Tragedian * Sir Peregrine Maitland (1777-1864) - Comm 1st & 2nd Bn Grenadier Gds at Waterloo. Gov Gen Upper Canada. Gov Cape Of Good Hope. * Florence Marryat (1838-99) - Writer, Playright,Actress, Opera Singer * Wm Calder Marshall (1813-94) - Sculptor * Chas Mathews (1803-1878) - Actor *Henry Mayhew (1812-87) - Writer on London's Poor. Originator of 'Punch' * Sir Wm Molesworth (1810-55) - Founded 'London Review.' * Earl of Mornington (d.1858) - Womaniser, Gambler & Rake * John Lothrop Motley (1814-77) - American Ambassador * Wm Mulready (1786-1863) - Artist. * John Murray (1778-1843) - Founder Publisher.* James Pope Hennessy (1916-74) - Writer * 5th Duke of Portland (1800-60) - Recluse Archt of underground buildings. * Dr Fredk Harvey Forster Quin (1799-1878) -1st homeopathic physician in England * Sir Terence Rattigan (1911-79) - Playwright * Giulio Regondi (1822-72) - Infant Concertina Prodigy * Jas Rendel (1799-1856) - Engr of docks worldwide * Sir John Rennie (1794-1874) - Civil Engr of London Bridge & Swedish Railways. Drainage of Lincolnshire fens * Jos Richardson (C.1790- 1855) - 'Inventor of The Rock,Bell & Steel Band' * Capt Chas Ricketts (1788-1867) - Joined Navy aged 7 under Nelson, Ret at 27.High Sheriff of Buckinghamshire * Richd Roberts (1789-1864) - Inventor * Sir Landon Ronald (1873-1938) - Musician. Accompanist to Dame Nellie Melba * Fredk August Rosen (1805-37) - Sanskrit scholar * Sir John Ross (1777-1856) - Naval explorer * Sir Chas Rowan (1783-1852) - Fought Peninsular War & Waterloo. Co-Founder of Metropolitan Police * Montagu Wm Lowery Corry (Lord Rowton) Secy to Disraeli * Wm Salter (1804-75) - Artist 'Waterloo Banquet' * Anne Scott (1803-33) - Daughter of Sir Walter Scott * Ed Scriven (1775-1841) - Helped to found Artists Benevolent Fund. * Edward Cator Seaton (1815-70) - Responsible for compulsory vaccination. * Sir Carl Wm Siemens (1823-83) - Metallurgist & Electrician, laid 1st transatlantic cable * Robt Wm Sievier (1794-1865) - Engraver, Sculptor Developer of Indiarubber & Wireless Telegraphy * Francois Simonau (1783-1869) - Painter - 'The Flemish Murillo' * Sir Geo Thos Smart (1776-1867) - Conducted music at funeral of George IV & Coronations of William IV & Queen Victoria * Robt Smirke (1752-1845) - Painter, Revolutionary George III refused to allow Royal Academy Keepership * Rev Jas Smirnove (1756-1840) - 60 Years Chaplain to Russian Embassy * Owen Smith (1809-79) - Bareknuckled Pugilist, opponent died after 85 rounds * Rev Sydney Smith (1771-1845) - Clergyman.Radical. Wit. * Jacob Sneider(D1866) - Inv breech loading rifle * Princess Sophia (1777-1848) - Daughter of George III * Alexis Benoit Soyer (1809-58) - Pioneer in mass catering, set up kitchens in Irish famine & Crimean war * Elizabeth Emma Soyer (1813-42) - Artist wife Of Alexis. * Alan Gibson Steel (1858-1914) - Cricketer, second only to W.G.Grace * Harriet Marian Stephen (1840-75) - Thackeray's daughter. m Sir Leslie Stephen 1st man up Mont Blanc. * Sir Jas Stephen (1789-1859) - Under Sec of State for the Colonies, where he abolished slavery. * Sir Jas Fitzjames Stephen (1829-94) - High Court Judge in trial of Wm Price cremating his son * Chas James Stewart (1775-1837) - Bishop of Quebec * Wm Strang (1859-1921) - Artist * Geo Augustus Smythe, Viscount Strangford (1818-57) 'A splendid failure'. last duellist in England. Model for Disraeli's 'Coningsby' * John McDougall Stuart (1815-66) - Explorer.1st to Cross Australia coast to coast * Sir Paul Strzelecki (1796-1873) Climbed & gave name to Australia's highest mountain * Augustus Frederick Duke of Sussex (1773-1843) 3rd son of George III. 'Married' twice in contravention of Royal Marriages Act * Dwarkanauth Tagore (d.1846) Indian poet * Wm Makepeace Thackeray (1811-1863) - Writer * Mary Ann Thurston (1810-1896) - Nurse to Queen Victoria's children * Teresa Caroline Tietjens (1831-1877) - Soprano * Sir Nicholas Conynham Tindal (1776-1846) - Lawyer, Counsel for Queen Caroline * John Lawrence Toole (1830-1882) - 'The last of the low comedians' * Anthony Trollope (1815-1882) - Writer. Postal reformer * Louisa Twining (1820-1912) - Reformer * Lucia Elizabeth Vestris (1797-1836) - Actress Soprano * Thos Wakely (1795-1862) - Politician. Founder of 'The Lancet' * Wm Vincent Wallace (1813-65) - Composer, pianist, guitarist, violinist & clarinetist. Saved from New Zealand savages by Chief's daughter * Jas Ward (1769-1859) - Painter, particularly of horses * John Wm Waterhouse (1849-1917) - Painter.'Hylas & The Nymphs' * Sir Fredk Watson (1773-1852) - Master of Household to George IV, William IV & Queen Victoria * Fredk Martin Jos Welwitsch (1806-72) - Keeper of Botanic Gardens, Lisbon * Wm Whiteley (1831-1907) - Founder, Whiteley's Store, murdered self-proclaimed illegitimate son * Horace Hayman Wilson (1780-1860) - Orientalist, 1st Sanskrit/ English Dictionary * Maj Chas Walter Clopton Wingfield (1833-1912) - Invt of Lawn Tennis * Fredk Albert Winsor (1783-1830) - Brought gas lighting to London. (Memorial only) * Jas Wyld (1812-87) - Cartographer. Creator of 'Wyld's Globe' 60'x40' & illuminated by gas.

Caryatids for Major-General Sir William Casement

touches it and removes the bandages of everyday life.' There was once a bench beside the grave on which Churchill would come and mourn. Many destroyed or stolen memorials remain as sorry traces, although the excellent Friends of Kensal Green are now restoring the place with every day that God gives them. Thanks to them the Dissenters' Chapel catafalque is once again in working order, enabling visitors to sink into the sombre beauty of the catacombs below. There, countless coffins – sparkling jewel-like from the rust of their ornate handles – are piled high behind Gothic grills. Covered with purple and scarlet velvets and leather, many are emblazoned with copper coronets or angels and others have brass plaques incised flowingly by the calligrapher's hand. Sir William Beatty – Lord Nelson's surgeon at

Trafalgar – is buried here, as is Henry Mayhew, the great chronicler of the London poor. The 5th Duke of Portland, who spent his life building underground, must feel happy to have ended his days in these subterranean vaults.

Among the galaxy of stars that inhabit these fifty acres, one who shines bright is Blondin the tightrope walker who was buried beneath a pink granite monument with portrait medallions of both him and his wife. His renowned feat was to cross the Niagara Falls on a one-thousand-foot-long tightrope in 1859. He repeated it blindfold and then on stilts. His poor manager was borne over on Blondin's back, and then pushed over in a wheelbarrow. The final triumph was to stop half-way across and, armed with a small stove, cook and eat an omelette!

One of the most splendid monuments in the cemetery – a vast canopy supported by Eastern caryatids –

MUSICAL BOUQUET

("THE OLD WATER MILL.")   ("WINTER.")

THE OLD ARM CHAIR.

THE BEAUTIFUL BALLAD BY ELIZA COOK _ THE MUSIC COMPOSED & SUNG BY HENRY RUSSELL.

ANDANTE CON ESPRESS:

I love it, I ... chide me for loving that

382. Musical Bouquet.
N.B. This much admired Ballad is published in the MUSICAL BOUQUET with the exprefs sanction of Mifs Eliza Cook, the writer of the words, and Mr. Henry Rufsell, the Composer of the Music, and is the authorised edition.

belongs to Major General Sir William Casement who met a mournful end. After serving in India for forty-seven years and six months, he was 'swayed by a sense of duty to defer his departure ... and terminated his valuable life at Cossipore in 1844'. It is a life which has continued after death, with many of those who were with him in India – including two heroes of the Mutiny – lying within earshot today.

Often though, it is the most remarkable characters that have the most modest memorial and vice versa. For example, John St John Long, a 'quack' doctor, has an immense Grecian monument with a dome covering a draped female figure. Claiming to have hit upon a cure for consumption by applying corrosive liniments and friction, he himself was to die of the disease, having steadfastly refused to apply his own cures.

James Barry, on the other hand, who lies under a most ordinary headstone had the most extraordinary life. He was, in fact, a woman who spent her life in the army, starting as a hospital assistant in 1813 and rising through the ranks – acting as surgeon with all the pre-anaesthetic horrors – to become Inspector-General. Lord Albemarle described '[him] as the most wayward of men; in appearance a beardless lad ... there was a certain effeminacy which he was always striving to overcome. His style of conversation was greatly superior to that one usually heard at the mess in those days.' 'He' was often accused of breaches of discipline and even fought a duel when stationed at the Cape.

The most fitting reminder of all the lives that are commemorated in Kensal Green is a small stone armchair. It was carved in honour of Henry Russell, the composer of such immortal melodies as 'Life on the Ocean Wave'. He wrote some 800 tunes including 'O Woodsman Spare That Tree' and most pertinently of all 'The Old Armchair'.

And so the roll call of honour goes on, with as many notables within these walls, it seems, as there are blades of grass. It is indeed a celestial congregation of characters that are gathered together at Kensal Green.

James Barry – in fact,
a woman

LOVED ONES

ARCHITECTURE can be put to no better purpose than the commemoration of those we love. Such shrines have been built all over the British Isles – memorable manifestations of mournfulness.

Occupying an oasis among the brutal blocks of a housing estate in London's East End, slashed through by underpasses and overpasses, lives a surprising if not unique artist called David Harrison who has created the most startling of shrines. You are shocked into wonder, having plodded up a grim concrete stairwell, past floor after floor of stench-ridden gloom, when suddenly – abracadabra – there is a white picket fence and latch gate entwined by a bower of blooms. Step inside and Bow seems a thousand miles away.

David Harrison is not so much a breath as a gale of fresh air, howling with delight each day at a thousand sights and sounds, while lacing everything through with uncommon niceness and hilarious originality. With an instinctive passion for architecture and art as well as nature, music and tat, he

The Mussenden temple on the bleak, bold shores of Derry

delights as much in the cheap charms of Barbie Doll's purple plastic handbag as in the subtlety of a medieval wall painting and, if a bird flies by or a dog hoves into view, they too are greeted with the same rapturous relish. To the wrath of animal rights supporters, he died his poodle fluorescent pink and, for one colourful spell, Hoover was decked out in purple fur with orange and yellow spots. When his canine friend died a shrine was built to its memory in the golden-walled dining room of the flat where they had lived for ten years. Hoover's ashes are in a musical china poodle, held on high by a golden cherub, while overall there is a gilded hand – which according to David belongs to Jayne Mansfield, 'the patron saint of poodles', gathering the soul up to a polystyrene heaven. Hoover's portrait blazes bright, surrounded by cherubs. 'I would have loved poodle cherubs,' laments David. A puce Venus de Poodle stands by a golden box of tissues 'for crying over the sad affair' and Hoover's diamanté collar and lead lie in a china box. 'I wanted the essence of him ... he knew what he liked and did not like. In his more sombre moods, even with music, he loved the *pas de*

The Empress – 'each day a bead on the rosary of life'

gilds or glitzes up to the nines and applies to the work in hand. 'I made a sad old thing of a wardrobe into an object of beauty by painting it silver and giving it a Chrysler Building top with garpoodles.' As a friend of his said, 'David is pure gold dust.'

On the bleak and bold shores of County Derry in Northern Ireland, there stands a very different memorial, the Mussenden Temple that clings to the cliffs at Downhill. It was a library built by Frederick Augustus Hervey, the disreputable Bishop of Derry and 4th Earl of Bristol, in honour of his young cousin Mrs Fridewide Mussenden who had died in 1785 when she was only twenty-two years old. It was, wrote the Bishop's biographer William S. Childe-Pemberton, 'a memorial to a lovely woman cut off in her prime and of the Bishop's romantic tribute to her perfection'. With 'her innocent spirits of eternal springs and cloudless skies' she was a source of endless joy to the Bishop, giving him 'slumbers sweet and spirits light' at the end of every happy day spent in her company, and causing him to bound out of bed each morning at dawn, after an hour of 'voluptuous meditation' over one of his innumerable and extravagant schemes. One such was the great house at Downhill built only yards from the temple, on a perishing prominence over the Atlantic, picturesquely reclaimed from moorland by the Bishop. Now a gaunt ruin, in its heyday the house was hung with paintings by Rembrandt, Titian, Poussin and Raphael. It was a bastion of elegance against the elements, with the servants being forced daily by the winds to crawl in and out on their hands and knees. The Bishop of Derry was an extraordinary figure, whose excesses were legendary, a colourful cauldron of good and bad, from philanthropy at its most pious to womanizing at its most wanton. His name was, in fact, scandalously linked with Mrs Mussenden but from reading his letters about 'her dear innocent

deux from the "Nutcracker Suite" especially … it reminds me so much of him.

'When I was a slave to them I always thought of poodles as Gods and Goddesses. I had plans to give great canine moquettes to the council to stand at their mortuary doors.' David creates and recreates his fantastical surroundings, using any old scraps picked up either for a song or off the street which he then countenance' and of him listening like a 'bon papa' to her improvements on the harpsichord, it would seem that the friendship was every bit as pure as the temple it commemorates. It is a perfect domed rotunda. Corinthian columns – all bored to act as drainpipes – march round the body of the building, beneath a frieze incised with an inscription from Lucretius: ''Tis pleasant, safely to behold from shore, the rolling ship and hear the tempest roar.'

The Bishop of Derry was a Protestant with great and active sympathy for the Catholics – Horace Walpole said that his popish sympathies qualified him for a cardinal's hat. Mass was said in the crypt beneath the floor of the Mussenden Temple and he helped with the building of many churches of both denominations throughout Derry. A builder on a grand scale, he created not only palaces and houses (Ickworth in Suffolk is a giant winged version of the Mussenden Temple as was to be the sadly unfinished Ballyscullion House in Derry) but also an abundance of bridges and monuments. His road works alone were likened to those of a Roman emperor rather than an Irish bishop.

Much of his time was spent in Europe buying paintings from contemporary artists and becoming the lover of all their wives. Each of these mistresses was then painted as Venus to hang on his walls. Descriptions of him in Rome are well worth recording: 'He was a reprobate with profane conversation … a little man with a face that is very sharp and wicked, and on his head, a purple velvet night cap with a dangling tassel of gold and a mitre to the front; he wore … a short round petticoat … fringed with gold about the knees … he looked like a witch while always giving himself the airs of Adonis. He is the strangest being ever made and with all the vices and foibles of youth, a drunkard and an atheist, though a Bishop, constantly talking blasphemy or indecency at

The Prince Imperial, who died his body bare save for Napoleon's seal and one sock

least, and at the same time very clever and with infinite wit. He courts every young and every old woman he knows.'

A Madame Ritz was one, to whom he wrote letters that showed 'a shameless disregard for his profession and ordinary morality'. He also courted a 'Mrs H… in whose large blue eyes a thousand cupids lay in ambush'. His name was entwined too with Lady Hamilton, although it would appear not romantically. He wrote that God must have been in a good mood when he created her. Lady Hamilton's description of the Bishop, that 'he is very entertaining and dashes at everything', gives a most pleasing picture of the man.

At Downhill, 'with the magnificent ocean roaring in a most authoritative tone', his days were spent with flourish. He entertained lavishly and in a manner that was 'highly characteristic of his whimsical humour', with such larks as sprinkling talcum powder down the bedroom corridors so as to trace the routes taken by philandering guests. On a summer's evening in 1784, he organized equestrian races on the beach between portly Anglican clergymen and trim Presbyterian ministers. The Presbyterians won the lot, after most of the Anglicans had fallen off their mounts, with the Bishop 'laughing heartedly at the discomforture of the church'. Another race was held with the prize of a valuable living when all the fattest clergy in the county were invited to run along what was, unbeknown to them, a stretch of quicksand. As they struggled even further, so they sank ever deeper, to the delight of the Earl Bishop.

It is, though, to the Earl Bishop's buildings that we must bow. They move one today every bit as much as they did a poet contributor to the *Belfast News-Letter* in the 1700s:

> *Whilst by the magic touch of Bristol's hand*
> *A new Creation springs at his command,*
> *And o'er naked waste and barren plain,*
> *Where nature mourn'd her unassisted reign,*
> *Now the fair dome in swelling order shews,*
> *The spire ascends and winding current flows;*
> *Who makes (the first great purpose of his breast)*
> *A country polish'd and a people blest.*

French flamboyance flies into the skies in Hampshire. After mile upon military mile, beside a roaring roundabout and behind a garish garage forecourt, you find yourself suddenly steeped in green and perfect peace. It is St Michael's Abbey in Farnborough where a mausoleum of ornate Gallic gothicary shelters the tomb of the last Emperor and Empress of France as well as their son Louis Napoleon, the Prince Imperial, who was slain by the Zulus.

It was built in 1887 by the architect Hippolyte Alexandre Gabriel Walter Destailleur for the Empress who in only eight years – between 1871 and 1879 – had lost an empire, a husband and a son.

She was born in Grenada – during a thunderstorm and an earthquake – the daughter of a Scotswoman and a Spaniard. Her life was to soar to the supreme splendours of the Second Empire, then sink to the ignominy of exile. It was her husband who, with Prefect Haussmann, was responsible for the mighty transformation of Paris. They rebuilt what was described as 'the nightmare cut-throat alleys of the Cité, the unkempt and unlighted Champs-Elysées… the undrained and filthy fever-haunted by-ways and the dusty neglected Bois. These were the excrescences and plague spots through which the Emperor drew his pencil.' Paris was gouged and gorged with new buildings. The Emperor who first hauled France into an ecstasy of pride and then wretchedly participated in her downfall following her humiliating defeat in the Franco-Prussian War at Sedan. Riding into battle – in piercing pain from stones in the bladder – with his fourteen-year-old son, he would sometimes be in the saddle for twenty-eight hours on end and without food. As always in his absence, the Empress of the French acted as Regent and when final defeat came, trapped in the Tuileries at the mercy of the mob, she ordered her husband not to return to Paris, writing that if he did he would be pelted with ordure rather than stones.

Her exceptional life can be grasped in the palm of your hand, as it were, when you gaze upon the assembly of objects that have survived. They belong to St Michael's Abbey but are temporarily on loan to the Aldershot Military Museum.

In 1858 there was an attempt to assassinate the Emperor by Orsini the Italian anarchist. (In fact, Napoleon III only got a scratched nose and a hole in his hat.) Among a number of bombs thrown outside the Opéra, one was somehow saved and is now safe in Hampshire, heavy as lead, surrounded with spikes and made in Birmingham. By its side are the locks of the Emperor's and the Prince Imperial's hair as well as the Emperor's hat and truncheon used when he was a young man living in England and acted as a Special Constable in the Chartist Riots of 1840.

Most remarkable of all are the shells that were fired, and the crumbs of bread that were saved, from the terrible siege of Paris. As the Tuileries were stormed, the Empress was forced to flee, racing through the galleries of the Louvre and into the improbable arms of an American dentist, a Mr Evans, who smuggled her to Deauville. He described the scene as the Empress left France, perhaps forever, 'with no flags, no cries of *Vive l'Impératrice ...* only the clouds in their black masses spread over the heavens like mourning drapery'.

The most poignant of the mementoes is the Prince Imperial's death mask as well as the strangely soft leaves that were gathered by the Empress from the spot where he was slain by the Zulus. He was her beloved and only child – such was the joy at his birth

(right) Bread from the Tuileries, Orsini's bomb, Napoleon's carriage shutters etc

that the Emperor and Empress declared themselves godparents to all 'legitimate' children born on the same day – who had been determined to prove his worth by fighting on the field. It was his mother, aided by Queen Victoria, who eventually persuaded Disraeli to let him go. '…The will of two obstinate old women,' lamented the Prime Minister. On 1 June 1879 the Prince's scouting party was ambushed by the Imbazani River. As he leapt into the saddle to escape, the girth snapped and he was hurled to the ground to face his fate. Fighting with Napoleon Bonaparte's sword he was done to death with seventeen plunges of the assegai spear. One was through the eye, as can be seen on the death mask. His body was found the next day, stripped bare save for Napoleon I's seal on a

chain around his neck and with one sock embroidered with the royal 'N' lying nearby. 'It was a sad sight,' wrote Major Grenfell. 'We his English brother officers stood round the dead body of the hope of the Imperialists of France.' The Empress sat white and motionless as a statue for some hours after hearing of the death of her son. He had met his maker with the 'bravery of a lion', the very words used by the Zulus who had killed him. 'My grief,' wrote Empress Eugénie, 'is animal, uneasy, angry … I bless every day that passes, simply for the reason that it has passed, it is a bead on the rosary of life, and what a life!'

And so, the legend that began in the scorching wilds of Corsica was to end in the cosy domesticity of Hampshire in England.

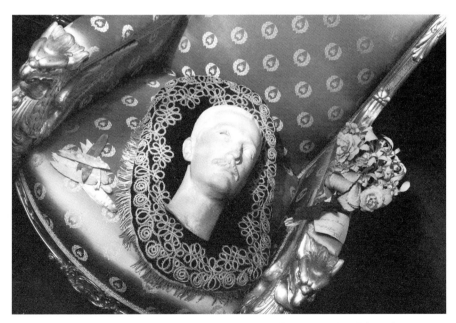

The death mask, his mother's funeral bouquet and the 'strangely soft leaves'

M25

HERE is a necklace of jewels strung around London, otherwise known as the M25. The motorway that causes misery and mayhem to so many is, in fact, surrounded, as it cuts through the countryside, by a collection of historical and architectural diversions which should provide the richest ruminations to all those stuck in a traffic jam, knowing that they are only tantalizing yards away from some tremendous treasure.

At Egham in Surrey, for example, pinnacled and pepper-potted towers, spires and domes, fanciful chimneys and finials all rise ebulliently out of the trees, giving the M25 its most stupendous skyline. It is Holloway College, a gargantuan château in Portland stone and 'flaming red brick' that 'fairly scorched the eye' when it was built between 1879 and 1887 by William Crossland for Thomas Holloway. It still screeches forth today; indeed when faced with its vivid vastness there seems no other building as bright and as big – 550 feet by 376 feet – in the whole world. Designed to attract the attention of the passing public on the railways, it reigns triumphant over the speeding motorway today. Thomas Holloway, 'one of the wonders of the 19th century', made millions with his 'healing genius' for inventing all-purpose pills and ointments; indeed so all-purpose were his remedies that one Irish farmer claims to have regained not only the use of all his limbs, his sight and his hearing but to have been relieved as well from pains plaguing him for twenty years. Truth to tell Holloway's genius lay in rhetoric rather than remedies, with his 'ample directions' as to how to take his medicines being translated into Sanskrit, Chinese, Armenian, Turkish, Arabic and most of the vernaculars of India. He became a great philanthropist, always claiming to have worked harder spending his money than in making it. Holloway College is proof of that pleasurable pudding: self-promotion and philanthropy on a monumental scale.

Nearby there is yet further endorsement of such excellence with the Holloway Sanatorium, built as a 'hospital for the insane of the middle class … and with grounds … equal to those at the Crystal Palace'. Today it has transmogrified into an 'exclusive' housing development. Grid-locked motorists should give three hearty cheers nevertheless for the preservation of its Franco-Flemish Gothic forms, crow-stepped gables, and great tower, modelled on the Cloth Hall at Ypres.

Near Cobham some eight miles to the south and off at Junction 10 there is Silvermere Haven, a pet cemetery with some hundreds of melancholy epitaphs, set in idyllic, undulating woodland and open fields. 'Gone for Long Walkies' must have

Holloway College – 'no building in the world seems so big'

ROYAL HOLLOWAY COLLEGE, EGHAM, SURREY.
OPENED HER LATE MAJESTY QUEEN VICTORIA, JUNE, 1886.

THE HOLLOWAY SANATORIUM, Virginia Water, Berks.
OPENED BY THEIR MAJESTIES THE PRESENT KING & QUEEN, JUNE, 1885.

THOMAS HOLLOWAY
The founder of the ROYAL HOLLOWAY COLLEGE & HOLLOWAY SANATORIUM the original Proprietor of
HOLLOWAY'S PILLS & OINTMENT.

wrought many a sad smile, as must the words commemorating Arabella the Irish Wolfhound: 'Gone to rest a while beside the gate, to await her master and her mate'. Another dog's tombstone is complete with three stone rabbits on its green glass chippings and the verse:

> *Willy's life went rushing by,*
> *Two years old when he died,*
> *I hope my Will's*
> *Somewhere around*
> *Chasing rabbits underground.*

(right) 'Gone for long walkies'

The cemetery, opened in 1977 by the Gilbert family, has undoubtedly brought solace to grieving pet owners who do not want their old companions simply to vanish without trace. Among the animals cremated or buried at Cobham are a twelve-foot-long python, two pigeons, two goldfish, and a dog and a rabbit in the same coffin. The tiniest interment was a cremation casket for a budgerigar and the largest was for Andy Parker, a seventeen-stone Irish Wolfhound who was so enormous that an MFI cupboard had to be bought as a coffin for the burial. His stone reads: 'Andy Parker Wolfhound. A true Friend and a Kind and loveable Gentleman 13–5–71 to 11–4–79'. A family of rats, too, have been buried in this paradisial resting place, with 'Gladstone – a Loving Rat' and 'Disraeli – a Kind Rat'. Also there is a terrapin, 'Shelly – a Lovely Reptile'.

I saw a cat's funeral at Silvermere Haven, with a tiny coffin arriving in a full-size hearse which had been driven at walking pace from Kingston. A solemn procession of two black-coated undertakers – one in a top hat – bore the little body to its grave. Every week one couple feel bound to come from Bournemouth, to stay for two days and tend their dog's grave. It is as spick and span as can be and ablaze with neatly planted flowers and shrubs, as is the whole of this poignant place.

A mere mile across the fields at Chaldon in Surrey, between Junctions 6 and 7, is the late twelfth- and early thirteenth-century church of St Peter and St Paul. Reached by a narrow-as-your-car road and presenting a particularly rural picture with its little flint body and wooden spire, it is the proud possessor of one of the rarest wall paintings in Europe. Dating from 1200, painted in the subtlest of colours, this presents a most gruesome scene, with little naked bodies scrambling up the Ladder of Salvation on their fearsome progress through Hell and Purgatory to Christ in the clouds on high. Beneath the serpent-entwined Tree of Knowledge, two three-toed giants torment deceitful tradesmen – the blacksmith without his anvil and the potter and spinning women without their wheels – by forcing them to perch on a saw of sharply symbolic spikes. Beneath them, roasting in flames and tortured by devils with hot irons, is the usurer laden with money bags and with coins pouring from his mouth. 'Lust' is represented by man and woman embraced by the devil; 'Envy' is a bald-pated figure longing for another's lustrous locks. Devils boil murderers in a cauldron and are about to pluck two more from the ladder and pitch them into the pot. She with the sin of 'Pride' is having her arm gnawed off by a beast. 'Gluttony' drains a bottle, whilst the figures of 'Sloth' walk on the back of an animal rather than making their own way. In Purgatory, the Archangel Michael is weighing the souls of the good and the bad, whilst a devil, having roped the damned together, tries to tip the scales with their weight. In the end it is God who triumphs, standing over the Devil rendered powerless – symbolized by tied hands – and consumed by flames.

In Kent the M25 thunders over the very stretch of railway line that inspired E. Nesbit to write *The Railway Children*. As a child she had lived at nearby Halstead and played on this track with her brothers. It was here, she said, that in her mind's eye the three children, Roberta, Peter and Phyllis, had had their great adventure. This was the spot where, by waving flags cut from the girls' red flannel petticoats, they had stopped the train from crashing into a landfall – when the ground had moved and the trees 'like the woods in *Macbeth*' had appeared 'to be walking slowly down the railway line'. It had seemed like 'magic' and they 'always knew that this railway line was enchanted'. Also beneath the motorway is a tunnel, the same one from which the trains would rush 'like dragons from their lairs', fanning the children with their 'hot wings' as they passed. It is here, too, where the trains sped by with all the passengers waving their hands, handkerchiefs and newspapers, making it 'fluttery and white, like pictures of the King's Coronation'. It seemed, wrote E. Nesbit, as if the train was alive, and was 'at last responding to the love that they had given it so freely and for so long'. How

joyless it is to think of the same book written today – with *The Motorway Children* waving away as their beloved juggernauts and cars roar past.

Sweeping over the elegant lines of the new Dartford Bridge, I am drawn down the Thames to Gravesend where Pocahontas lies buried. She was my seven times great-grandmother and it was thanks to her support in the 1600s that the early English settlers

Roberta, Peter and Phyllis waving handkerchiefs and red flannel petticoats beneath where the M25 thunders today

in America were able to survive. (Woe betide the Disney version today.) As you speed the full circle of the M25 you can hoot a salute in honour of so many who lie buried on either side. Delius, the composer, as well as his champion Sir Thomas Beecham and the pianist Eileen Joyce are all buried at St Peter's at Limpsfield in Surrey. Nearby at West Horsley you can ponder over the remains of the executed Sir Walter Raleigh's head, which lies beneath the floor of the chapel of St Mary's Church. When his body was buried at St Margaret's, Westminster, his desolate wife had his head embalmed and kept it with her – in a red leather bag – until the day she died. St Michael's Church at St Albans harbours the body of Sir Francis Bacon, the philosopher, whose wisdom it was said was 'too far in advance of the time to be palatable'. And it was this very advanced wisdom that brought about his demise in 1626. Determined upon experimenting with his notion of freezing food he had scrabbled about in the snow, packing a chicken carcass on Highgate Hill, where he caught a chill and within days had perished from bronchitis. The spot where King Harold lies buried is at Waltham Abbey in Essex; while there is a royal connection of the most harrowing kind among the ruins of the Dominican priory at Kings Langley in Hertfordshire. Piers Gaveston, Earl of Cornwall, lies there, and it was thanks to his doubtful connection with Edward II that in 1327 the King was hideously done to death with a red-hot poker at Berkeley Castle in Gloucestershire, his screams, it was said, being audible from two miles' distance.

A far happier spot is the pristine, perfect, little Quaker Meeting House at Jordans, burial place of William Penn, the august Quaker and founder of Pennsylvania. When the apple trees are in full blossom and the greensward glints in this intrinsically English scene, it is strange to think of another memorial to Penn, perched high on Philadelphia's City Hall: a life-size statue which planning laws prevented from being superseded by a taller building until the late 1980s.

The roll call of honour around the M25 need never end. The remains of Anthony Hope, author of *The Prisoner of Zenda*, lie at Leatherhead and those of Martin Secker – founder of Secker and Warburg, the first publishers of D.H. Lawrence – are at Iver in Buckinghamshire. Most imposing of all is Wyatt's monument to Thomas Gray at Stoke Poges, in a little enclosure near to the churchyard of St Giles, the inspiration for his 'Elegy in a Country Churchyard' and the place where he himself is buried.

The modest exterior of St Mary's Church at Great Warley in Essex gives only a few clues – such as the fanciful Art Nouveau drainpipe heads – to the orgy of opulence within. Open the door and the altar seems to explode with its blindingly brilliant aluminium-coated apse that frames the most elegant row of trees in the kingdom. Their brass roots clench around green marble, their trunks rise up to bear red glass pomegranates and mother-of-pearl roses, while in their branches there are angels of oxidized silver, standing in graceful rigidity and bearing such banners as 'Joy' and 'Peace'. This is the lustrous rood screen, shown as a work of art in the Royal Academy in 1903, which was designed – as was the interior – by Sir William Reynolds Stevens. The organ case is built in an array of different metals and with the cosiest of countryside scenes beaten into burnished brass. Everywhere you look the scene shines before you, right down to the detailing of all the light fittings and door handles. Christ clad in silver and mother-of-pearl stands above all behind the altar, his robes alive with varying glints. Bronze angels envelop the font, the pulpit is of beaten copper, and the reading desk, in

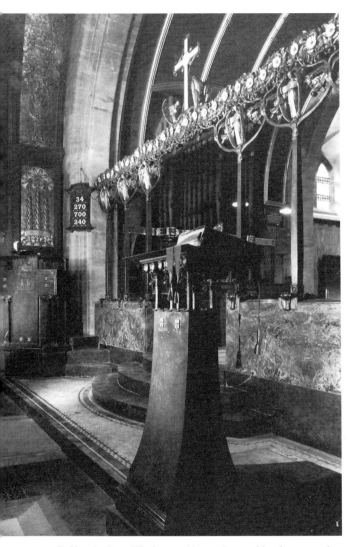

St Mary's, Great Warley – as if a magic wand has been waved

true Art Nouveau style, smoothly sweeps up from the floor. It is as if a magic wand has been waved with the wish that all around be transformed into treasure.

Rearing up over the thundering carriageways –

between Junctions 25 and 26 – there is a fire-gutted classical pile with windows that give the appearance of gouged-out eyes staring sightlessly over the traffic below. It is Copped Hall in Essex, built in 1751 by John Sanderson, and partly decorated by Robert Adam. Subsequently, it was richly re-embellished, first in the 1770s by James Wyatt and again in the late nineteenth century by Charles Eamer Kempe – the most romantic stained-glass artist of his day. As you gaze up at the roofless ruin, you can reflect upon rooms that once dripped with pendanted painted ceilings and walls richly panelled, inlaid and columned with wood.

But it was the late nineteenth-century gardens of Copped Hall that were most startling, sweeping off on an ornamental shelf into the Essex countryside. Statues stood atop carved columns, rising out of octagonal fountains and two summerhouses vied in grandiosity with the house itself, the separate ballroom building and the conservatory. The gardens, with a spiky skyline of at least a hundred obelisks and yard upon yard of stone balustrading decorated with urns and balls, were not to everyone's taste. 'A suspicion of restraint,' wrote one critic, 'would greatly have improved the general effect.' Sadly it has almost all disappeared today. Stare hard though and certain outlines can be traced.

A great Tudor house once stood on this estate and was demolished in 1751. It had been given to Sir Thomas Heneage by Queen Elizabeth in 1564 and it is here that the Catholic Mary Tudor was made a virtual prisoner by the Protestant King. In 1595 these grounds were witness to the wedding celebrations of Sir Thomas and his second wife, the Countess of Southampton, for which Shakespeare wrote *A Midsummer Night's Dream*. The play was performed at Copped Hall for the very first time, within yards of what is now the M25.

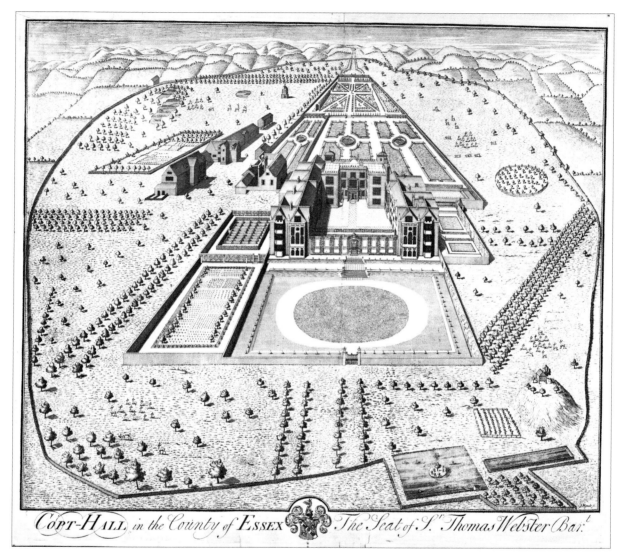

COPT-HALL in the County of ESSEX   The Seat of S.ᵗ Thomas Webster Bar.ᵗ

A Midsummer Night's Dream *was first performed here*

It is known, but has always been difficult to believe, that Temple Bar, that great stone archway that spanned The Strand, is to be found hidden away in a wood in Hertfordshire. Go to Theobalds Park and you will suddenly come upon it and, for good measure, be staggered by its size. It was designed by Sir Christopher Wren in 1672 to mark the western limit of the City of London and schemes are afoot to return it to a place of deserved glory in the streets of London today. Standing alone with this mighty beauty in a wood it is shiveringly sinister to dwell on what those stones have seen, including such horrors as the heads and bodies of traitors pushed on to high spikes for all to see. In 1684 the quartered corpse of Sir Thomas Armstrong was displayed in loathsome decay, having first been boiled in salt so as not to be eaten by birds. His head, curiously enough, was on view at Westminster Hall but those of his fellow conspirators, Lord John Russell and Algernon Sydney – they had plotted to kill King Charles II – were on show at Temple Bar. Telescopes could be hired for a halfpenny a look.

Temple Bar was hung with black velvet for Lord Nelson's funeral procession on 9 January 1806, when the Admiral's body was hauled through in a canopied ship on wheels. Festooned with fringing, drapes and plumes the great funeral car was hung with the Royal Ensign at half mast. Oh what an illustrious procession from the past could march beneath Temple Bar's arch.

So next time you are trapped in the traffic on the M25, remember the glories that are strung around it – a dazzling necklace of gems, indeed.

Temple Bar, now hidden away in a Hertfordshire wood

NOTTINGHAM'S PRIDE

T is seldom that you love a house as much as its owner, or an owner as much as his house. Flintham Hall in Nottinghamshire is an exception, where Myles Hildyard and his house both fused in flamboyant measure with a sense of adventure and originality.

He was thirteen when his family moved into Flintham, after his great-uncle had died in 1928. 'My mother used to dread coming here when he was alive with the old horse and brougham plodding out from Newark railway station. She thought the Midlands hideous having been brought up with primroses in Sussex.' Then there was the dark and dreary house 'which had entirely gone to ruins – surrounded by wellingtonias and full of hip baths'. Narrow strips of lino lay on all the floors, the sofas had all 'exploded' and the walls of the hall were lined with box upon box of stuffed birds piled on top of one another. 'There was also a naked statue,' says Myles, 'which was surprising as my great-uncle was so Godly. He was low church and spoke very very slowly … He sat in an overcoat in the freezing drawing room lit by a single gas flame at the end of a long red rubber pipe. At the end of every week he would send the money that he had saved by not having a fire to the Congo Mission – usually about two shillings and sixpence!' (His father had grotesquely overspent with two houses in Eaton Square – for his wife and his mistress.)

At Flintham Myles's miserly great-uncle would 'wrestle with God' every evening when in bed, overheard through the ventilating grill above the gasolier in the ceiling which acted like a microphone into the drawing room below. 'He would argue with God throughout the night, literally about what bull should be sent to what cow, or whether he should sell some pearls to the Red Cross!'

'Myles's mother should have shouted up, "It's God here, I advise you to give those pearls to your nephew's wife!"' says David Rowbottam, who lives at Flintham today with Myles, and is responsible for many of the house's marvels of restoration and reinvention. When Myles grew up in the house Flintham was considered 'hideous' and he can well remember being branded with the shame of living there.

Originally a deadly dull medieval and Jacobean gabled manor – relieved only by two Gothic windows – it was trimmed and mainly rebuilt into an even plainer box in 1798. This was enlarged by Lewis Wyatt in 1829 – his severe red-brick north front still stands today. Twenty-four years later, however, the rest of the house was transmogrified into a Victorian potentate's palace by the architect T.C. Hine. Encrusted with elaborately carved stone and crowned with a tower and balustrade, Flintham was enriched with an addition that even in its day was remarkable enough but has now become, by reason of its survival,

Flintham, with its diadem of a conservatory

quite unique. This glistening cherry on the cake is a gargantuan barrel-vaulted conservatory, the lunette of which was obviously inspired by the Crystal Palace (the Great Exhibition had taken place a few years earlier). It has a sturdy rather than spindly presence, in keeping with the rest of the house. With the solid use of identical stone between the glass, Flintham

and its conservatory diadem are united. It is the only great Victorian conservatory attached to a house still put to its original use. Joseph Paxton designed one for Capesthorne in Cheshire, measuring 150 feet by 50 feet, which was demolished around 1920. The vast winter garden of the 1850s at Somerleyton Hall in Suffolk has also been destroyed, and the conservatory built for the Rothschilds at Halton House in Buckinghamshire, which had two large and nine small

'A marble fountain covered with snakes, shells and flowers'

domes, as well as an adjoining skating rink has, alas, now gone.

Inside at Flintham the surprise comes when, taken unawares, you step into the Little Library – through a doorway designed to lead you in at its corner. On the far side, off axis with the door and across the small, dark and richly decorated room, a screen of columned arches beckons. Stand between the columns and you are thunderstruck. The sheer change of scale is enough, let alone the spellbinding rarity before your eyes. Rising up for two floors is the Big Library, alive with light from enormous windows as well as from the

conservatory beyond – seen in its jungle-like lushness through two storeys of arched windows. Along one wall of the library stands an immense town-hall-size fireplace in a style 'founded on that of the Cinquecento'. Designed by T. R. Macquoid for the Great Exhibition, it was bought by Thomas Blackborne Thoroton Hildyard in 1851, at a time when he had nowhere to put it. When it was finally installed in these magnificent surroundings it can have made little difference to the icy air. According to Myles, 'It must have been unheatable. Now it takes enough kilowatts to power a row of houses as well as a tree or two in the grate.' When home on leave from the war – he was awarded the MC for his heroism in the withdrawal from Crete – he was forced to wear a 'Russian bearskin ankle-length coat' in the room.

All around the library, at what should be ceiling level, there is a gallery reached by two stone spiral staircases, their entrances carved with such vignettes as a gardener with one leg in the air, holding a pot of fuchsias. Two enormous crystal gasoliers hang with fairy-like lightness from the ceiling. If you parade round the balcony above them, you arrive at what is perhaps the most joyous surprise of all: a balcony hanging over into the conservatory, from which you can gaze up at the thirty-foot-high blue and white plumbagos, as well as three begonias and a cobaea rampaging up the full height of the building. The walls are coated with mirrors on the east side giving the impression of boundless jungle; with tree ferns (one from Hawaii), mimosa, daturas, strelitzias, an abutilon (twenty feet high, although not a climber), a rhododendron 'Fragrantissima', orange and lemon trees and tibouchina – all of them growing from deeply dug beds. There are pots of hedychium (ginger plants) as well as lapageria, agapanthus, clivia and canna. A jasmine leaps twenty-five feet up the north wall. A marble fountain covered with snakes, shells and flowers tinkles down in three tiers. The barrel vault is forty feet high, built specifically for palms. (There were two when Myles was a child, which were cut down by his father but which still lie, soundly solid, in the garden.) Nine great counterweighted baskets – heavy as lead and bulging with blooms – are startling survivals. This fairyland was once lit by gas, shooting forth from iron stamens in porcelain lilies. Amid their bronze leaves sat the porcelain figure of Dorothea – another trophy from the Great Exhibition.

These wonders and a thousand others throughout the house were created by Myles's great-grandfather, whose confidence in the future was far greater than the contents of his coffers. His grandfather before him had led a colourful life, in the course of which he married Roosilia, the fifteen-year-old illegitimate daughter of the Duke of Rutland and the late Duchess's maid, Mrs Elizabeth Drake – a legendary beauty who, for once, looks the part in her portrait, staring out like a voluptuous swan. The household would sit at the table, the Duke at one end and Mrs Drake at the other, with their four children in between, waited on by Mrs Drake's brother who was still the Duke's valet and butler. It was her great-grandson who was to festoon Flintham in all its finery; with carved swags and stone balls in abundance on the outside, and with room after rich room within. Another curious detail was that he took away seven water closets and replaced them with only two. Two rare 'Tip-Up' basins by George Jenning (he who introduced the public lavatories to the world) survive in the house;

on a pivot, they are swung upside down to be emptied. There is an immense bath in the attic, big enough for six men to sit in, which at no point could have had any hot water, the tanks being woefully small and situated many hundreds of yards from the boilers in the basement. Myles Hildyard's contemporary contribution has been a shining oak bathroom as well as a swimming pool in the greenhouse, in which you float beneath a roof of vines and walls of geraniums. Michelangelo's *David*, who stands above, caused Myles terrible consternation on arrival at Flintham, having been mistakenly delivered to the church where he stood at the door, bright and white in all his nakedness, only removed, in the nick of time, just before the service began.

Myles, now eighty-two years old, is a farmer and aesthete with a zest for life that is matched by few a quarter his age. He is a curious combination: conventional without being the least conformist and a lover of tradition who thunders forward with innovative thought and action. He has given his life to the house and, by successfully farming the land, has managed to haul Flintham from its gloomy past into a glorious present. 'There was never an alternative … all

through the war my letters home yearned for news of the snowdrops and Flintham.' His life of 'primroses, daffodils, and snowdrops, planning woodland walks and burying dogs' he says was not necessarily ideal and that 'it is a great sorrow not to have married and had children. Nevertheless,' he muses with a smile, 'my primroses are more reliable than drunken children.'

A gardener with one leg in the air

OPULENT ENDINGS

HE ancient art of building a mausoleum – that mansion of a monument in which to rest for eternity – was revived in the British Isles during the 1700s.

The word itself comes, incidentally, from Queen Artemisia's mighty chamber of death for King Mausolus in 355 BC – he was her beloved husband and, I'm afraid, her brother! The eighteenth-century revival was all part of a new understanding of antiquity which caused a craving for classical architecture. The mortuary monument, on its relatively modest and manageable scale, provided a Heaven-sent opportunity to emulate the buildings of Rome, Greece and Egypt while placing them piously and picturesquely in the landscape. So enthusiastically was this opportunity seized that Britain led most of Europe in building these neo-classical mausolea. Today though, it is no longer fashionable to pour cash into such commemorations. Those who could and would have done so in the past now set up charitable foundations in their self-perpetuating honour. Today's tycoon, alas, does not seek immortality with towering temples!

Cobham – now daubed with such slogans as 'DRUGS'

Nowhere is the demise of the mausoleum more searingly symbolic than at Cobham in Kent, where the classical ideal was realized by James Wyatt in 1783–4. An elegant little building for the Earl of Darnley, this classical temple topped with a pyramid is now a wretched ruin, fluorescently daubed with such slogans as DRUGS – an extreme example of a once vigorous architectural form now drained of life. There is one proposal afoot to convert it into a house.

As usual with such buildings there was a funeral chapel above the crypt. Lord Darnley's chapel once had a marble floor – there is no floor at all today – and there were pink marble columns about the walls, all shining with the light from the stained glass in the lunette windows. This graceful building was never consecrated. The Bishop of Rochester was to give it his blessing in the 1780s but instead had a blazing row with Lord Darnley and left before the holy deed was done.

Before the eighteenth-century revival of the classical mausoleum – designed as much to beautify the landscape as to honour the dead – affluent families had almost invariably built private chapels attached to churches in which to bury their loved ones. In north London at St Lawrence, Little

The mausoleum to Mausolus

Stanmore, there is a ravishingly beautiful example, created on the very cusp of the change – a classical chamber for the dead still comfortably clinging to the body of the church. It was built by James Gibbs, the 1st Duke of Chandos, in 1735 in honour of his second wife, Cassandra. Amid the subtle paintwork of *trompe-l'œil* trickery and grisaille – all by Gaetano Brunetti – the Duke stands bewigged and in full Roman rig attended by his devout spouses. Cassandra is on his left while his first wife, Mary, kneels on his right. Two more tombs were added later – to Margaret and Mary, the wives of the 2nd and 3rd Dukes of Chandos.

The Duke's vainglorious monument was carved twenty-seven years before he died. 'My Lord advances with majestic mien, Smit with the mighty pleasure to be seen,' wrote Alexander Pope in one of

'My Lord
advances with
majestic mien,
Smit with the
mighty pleasure
to be seen'

the many satires written on the man. As Paymaster-General to George I, Chandos had amassed a prodigious fortune and he speculated on a grand scale, providing Pope with yet more fodder:

Yet since just Heaven the Duke's ambition rocks,
Since all he got by fraud is lost in stocks.
… O! wert thou not a Duke my good Lord Humphry
From baliffe's claws thou scarce could keep thy bum free.

Much of the Duke's money, though, was spent to grand architectural effect, both on his mausoleum and on Canons, his palace nearby, where the staircase alone was made from twenty-two-foot-long slabs of marble. (After the house was demolished this ended up in the Odeon Cinema in Broadstairs, where it was blitzed during the war.) His private chapel was of singular magnificence with a full choir in permanent attendance, who would sing to the dining company every evening.

George Frederick Handel was the Duke's Master of Music and spent two years at Canons, when he wrote the twelve Chandos anthems, as well as his first English oratorio – *Esther*.

Beneath the mausoleum at Stanmore there is an especially sad crypt with a quantity of children's coffins all of softly sunken lead. Five of the 1st Duke's sons had died. Anne Wells, who married the 2nd Duke, is with them. It was said that he bought her for £20 from her former husband – a 'brutal ostler' who was offering her for sale on the streets of Newbury in the early 1740s.

The classical mausolea went on being built throughout the eighteenth and nineteenth centuries. Indeed one of the purest of all mausolea, looking especially like an ancient prototype, was designed in 1852 at Hamilton in Lanarkshire. It was for 'El Magnifico', the 10th Duke of Hamilton, described as

'the proudest man in Britain', who furthermore believed himself to be the rightful King of Scotland. Having inherited a gigantic fortune, he was to aggrandize his estates on an epic scale. His house, Hamilton Palace, was outrageously opulent. It was demolished in 1920 after mining had been allowed beneath its foundations. Considered the wonder of Scotland with an abundance of rare marbles and mosaics, the general effect was of 'most massive and princely splendour', wrote one visitor. Three of the rooms were dismantled to be rebuilt: one in Boston, another in Dallas and a third has just been returned to Scotland from the Metropolitan Museum in New York where it had been discovered in packing cases.

In death the Duke was determined to reign resplendent. The great domed drum was designed by David Bryce, with sculpture by Alexander Handyside Ritchie. (It is said that Ritchie was a 'hit and miss sculptor' and here he decidedly missed.) The stones of the Hamilton mausoleum were dovetailed together with the minimum of mortar but with such maximum success that, despite having a coal seam mined

Built for 'El Magnifico', the 10th Duke of Hamilton

beneath, it swayed and it sank but it never fell down. At the Duke's funeral in 1852, *The Times* wrote that the building 'is believed to be the most costly and magnificent temple for the reception of the dead in the world – always excepting the pyramids'. Inside, a marble, granite, porphyry and jasper floor reflects the architecture that soars overhead. Its centrepiece of a radiant star is lit directly from the cupola – 'the eye of God' – shining from above.

Although the Duke died before the building was completely finished, enough progress had been made for him to lie in his megalomaniac monument as his funeral service reverberated around him. Unfortunately a disastrous twenty-five-second echo had been discovered, rendering the service incomprehensible. Finally, the Duke was laid to rest in a sarcophagus of

Scots baronial set a-leaping in Arbroath

'utmost rarity' which he had originally bought on behalf of the British Museum. It was thought to contain the body of the Queen of Amasis, but when the remains were discovered instead to be those of a mere court jester called Irit-irw, the Duke refunded the money. On his last journey abroad he procured Eastern spices for his own embalmment, and would often try the sarcophagus out 'for size', albeit with singular lack of success since he had failed to take account of the obligatory lining and, when he died, his feet had to be cut off to crush him into his treasure. There are no longer any Hamiltons in the crypt. When the mining set the mausoleum trembling in the 1920s all the bodies were hauled off on coal carts to the cemetery nearby, where, incidentally, Sir Harry Lauder now lies but a stone's throw away.

At Arbroath in Angus, there is a mausoleum without precedent and without equal. It was built by Patrick Allan-Fraser of Hospitalfields to house his parents-in-law, his wife and himself for all eternity, and as a philanthropic gesture to give the town a mortuary chapel for their dead. The castle-revival style of Scotland, so often lumbering, has in this case been set a'leaping with towers, domes and spires all thrusting themselves heavenwards. It was begun in 1875 and continuously carved for the next twenty-five years by the stonemason James Peters of Arbroath. Local delights have been lauded in the red sandstone of Angus; rabbits peer from pillar capitals, cranes cross their bills in a most decorative way. There is a frog modelled from a corpse which had been brought in by children who asked for it 'to be built into the chapel'. Pillars are carved as tree trunks in a variety of barks and there are quantities of bulrushes, flowers and foliage – none of them the same – throughout the building. Every aspect of the mortuary chapel, even that which would never be seen, has been meticulously executed and unless you are rambling on the roof you will miss the most moving of all. There, all but hidden from view and marching around a little tower, is a humble Highland funeral – every figure bowed down with the grief. Both Patrick Allan-Fraser and his wife Elizabeth were worthy patrons of local life, nurturing the best of the artists and craftsmen of Angus. One most unexpected result was the bringing to life of Nanky Poo in *The Mikado* – first sung by the son of the Allan-Frasers' estate-manager whom they had sent to train as a tenor in Italy.

There are precious few twentieth-century mausolea in Britain but, strange to say, those with the most unbroken line to the classical past were built in the early 1900s at Brookwood Cemetery in Woking. They are the temples honouring the Parsees – originally the ancient Persians – who have preserved their Zoroastrian religion, in its pure form, for 3500 years. These three little buildings have been set down in 'paradise' – the ancient Persian word for garden – with plants that were all chosen because they still bear their Persian names: asparagus and spinach as well as jasmine, lilac and nectarine. These mausolea have a dash of magic – another word with its roots in the Magi of Persia – in that they are true classical temples, uncluttered by artifice, direct descendants of their ancient ancestors from 1500 BC.

It is sad, indeed, to realize that this architecture of death is all but a dead architecture today.

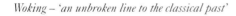

Woking – 'an unbroken line to the classical past'

PRISONERS OF WAR

JUST north of Wells in Somerset, grazed by the road to Midsomer Norton, there is the most curious classical monument. Blink and you will miss it. Catch a glimpse and you will not believe your eyes. Perched high on a podium are Romulus and Remus – the founders of Rome – suckling the she-wolf who mythically reared them. Roman to their roots and planted there in the soil of Somerset, they make the most surprising sight. Seemingly ancient, it is only when you peer closely and spot corroding iron protruding from collapsed cement that you realize they are relatively new. In fact, the monument was sculpted by an Italian prisoner of the Second World War, Gaetano Celestra, in gratitude for the happy times spent working on a farm in these parts owned by Mr Wellstead-White. 'I think the prisoners were happy to be in England,' says Mr White. 'They had been treated so badly in other countries, they were pleased to be thought of as human beings again.'

All round the British Isles such touching relics can be found, monuments which, once you know of their origins, speak intensely of the pride and pain of this particularly bitter form of expatriate life.

Most remarkable is what was achieved at Lambholm on Orkney, where several hundred Italian prisoners – captured during the North African campaign – spent the war building the concrete causeways to defend Scapa Flow. Living in a grim collection of huts known as Camp 60, they set about humanizing their surroundings with passion and panache. A theatre was created complete with painted scenery and a hut was reserved for recreation, for which they built a concrete billiard table. But the centrepiece was their chapel, built out of two bolted-together Nissen huts, with a pinnacled façade and a painted interior that would do credit to any Tuscan town. That such an exquisite little building should be created in such barren surroundings and bleak circumstances is surely as near a manifestation of a miracle as is possible.

One prisoner, a former artist, Domenico Chiocetti, was responsible for the design and, with the help of former cement worker Bruttapasta, created the elaborate Gothic exterior that springs forth from the slug-like bodies of the Nissen huts. Inside plasterboard encases all, painted to look like brick and sweeping round the semi-circular body of the chapel to be supported by a painted 'pierced stone' dado. 'Stone' vaults are painted on to the ceiling. The sanctuary screen was woven into a delicate web by prisoner Palumbo – a former ironsmith – who also forged two candelabra. Four more were made out of brass by prisoner Primavera. Many a peacetime profession came in handy: Bruttapasta was a cement worker who, as well as ecclesiastically cladding the exterior, created a concrete altar, altar rail and font – all polished to look like marble. The cement leftovers from the great barriers were given a second and most unexpected use. Ships, too, had been sunk in an attempt to create a defence and tiles from their lavatories were used to go round the altar of the chapel. Wood was salvaged for the tabernacle. High above sits Chiocetti's 'The Madonna of the Olives' who had been with him throughout the war, on a postcard in his pocket. The war ended before the chapel was finished but a special service was held, to the accompaniment of the bells and choir of St Peter's in Rome on a gramophone in the vestry. When the prisoners departed Chiocetti gallantly stayed on to finish his glories alone. He returned in 1960 and again in 1964 to the little chapel where he said he had left 'part of my heart'.

At Norman Cross, near Peterborough, by the side of the A1, there was once another prisoner of war camp, in 1797 the first one in the world to be purpose-built for the ever-increasing number of European captives (mostly French) of the Napoleonic Wars. The Governor's house still remains, as does a short stretch of its perimeter wall and, until recently, a bronze eagle perched on a pillar to commemorate the spot. This was stolen but plans are afoot to raise funds to replace it. What does survive, however – in the safe haven of the Peterborough Museum – is the peculiarly interesting collection of some 600 artefacts that were made by the prisoners between 1797 and 1815. They all reveal delightful dexterity and are, for the most part, decidedly odd. One shining white castle – made from bones from the cookhouse and polished and painted so as to seem like inlaid ivory – has a household of hundreds. Soldiers made from bones can be turned on a wheel so as to march on the

ramparts and there is a ballroom filled with revellers who can be made to dance. A carpenter planes his wood and a lady plies her pestle and mortar. This marvellous ornamentation is all the more amazing, considering that the castle – measuring three foot by four – was designed to do nothing other than house two fob watches. The prisoners made guillotines, too, out of their mutton bones. Fantastically complex in construction and manned by armies of uniformed soldiers, these are all gruesomely workable – with the heads of the aristocrats made of putty so they can be used over and over again. The workmanship was of the highest quality, with the French prisoners producing such refinements as 'Neptune's Kingdom' – an intricately carved assembly of creatures which seem, as always, to be of rarest ivory. An 'escritoire' of straw marquetry is as stylish as if inlaid with richest woods and a straw picture of Peterborough Cathedral is flawless, with every nuance of light and shade dancing through its Gothic detailing. So successful was the straw work at Norman Cross during the Sunday market in the prison that local traders complained that they were being outdone. The prisoners' straw hat making was declared illegal, as its excellence, as well as the fact that the hats were duty free, had knocked the bottom out of the British bonnet-making market! The poet George Borrow, describing Norman Cross as 'A sad cross to many a Norman', wrote of hearing the prisoners' cries of 'Vive l'Empereur' ringing out over the English countryside – yells of defiance at guards burning a quantity of straw hats already made. There were many escapes; one prisoner wrote of scarpering with 'an extra pair of stockings which I found most refreshing'. He had worn 'a good pair of strong shoes … another great comfort which ought to be particularly attended by every adventurous wanderer'.

With the defeat of Napoleon in 1815, the white

Grim guillotines of mutton bones

Bourbon flag was raised over each of the prison's four quadrangles as the captives danced and laughed, cried and sang with joy. The garrison, too, became infected with the delirium and out of sheer bravado dragged the Glasgow stage coach from nearby Stilton – horses, passengers and all – to join in the celebrations.

As an extra bonus Peterborough has another humdinger of an object made by a prisoner of war, this time by an Italian of the Second World War. It is an aluminium cigarette case of 'Jane' of the *Daily Mirror*, one side showing her clothes on and the other with them off – as the *Mirror* promised they would be when the War was won.

Most of the First and Second World War camps have disappeared – with few regrets – but at Island Farm near Bridgend in South Wales there has been the most exciting conservation clamp-down. Here – in some thirty grim buildings – German prisoners of war were housed between 1944 and 1948 and a preservation order has been put on an escape tunnel as well as the hut from which that escape was made. On 11 March 1945 sixty-six men got away – the sixty-seventh was spotted by his white kit bag and was shot in the shoulder. Working behind a false wall in the hut, the men dug a tunnel under the perimeter fence and, wonder of wonders, that tunnel is still there today. It is forty-five feet long and was excavated with hands, cans and knives. The prisoners were always naked so as not to have tell-tale earth on their clothes. All were caught; the first ones out were the last to be recaptured – rugger-tackled to the ground by a Welsh farmer. In the absence of a police station they were

Jane – clothed and in victorious nudity at the War's end

marched off to the local Post Office, for a genial tea with the post mistress. Their escape, they said, was 'good sport'. Most imaginatively, CADW – Welsh Historic Monuments – has listed the hut as a Grade II building along with the tunnel. Fragments of walls from other huts on Island Farm have also been saved, on which pin-ups were painted – haunting reminders of camp life and the glamorous companions who cheered them on each day. In 1946 no fewer than 127 German generals and field marshals were dispatched to Bridgend, most notably Field Marshal Gerd von Rundstedt, Chief of the German Army in the West, and General Carl Wolff, Himmler's Chief of Staff. When one group of German officers arrived at the local station, they refused to carry their cases the two miles to the camp. It was only with the appearance of Mr Hill the station master, resplendent in his uniform of long frock coat and gold-braided hat, that the officers would oblige – thinking that they had been given orders by a general! The camp site – save for the single hut and tunnel – is now a Science Park.

By far the most moving of all memorials to the spirit that shone through those dark days of the war is to be found at Henllan in South Wales. There among a sorry collection of huts is another Italian chapel, this time in dire and desperate need of funds but still clinging on to life as determinedly as were the prisoners who built it. '*Questa è la casa di Dio e la Porta del Cielo*','This is the House of God and the Doorway to Heaven' is painted above the door as you step inside, with your heart bleeding at the sight before your eyes. That such a building as this, created in times of singular strife, should have been so ravaged by times of peace is to be deplored. Mr Robert Thompson and his son Andrew have kept it standing – with minimal funds and maximum effort – but they cannot go on for much longer. Arches spring out from concrete columns, painted to look like marble and topped with

The House of God and the Doorway to Heaven

scrolls of old tin cans. The most ordinary materials have been used to extraordinary effect. Two side altars were built out of ration boxes and the dome over the main altar was made of cement on a wire frame. To give it sweep, the joists were cut through – undermining the structure. Hence Mr Thompson's desperate measure of roof props that march up the aisle today. All the paintings were applied on to

*'Bulgingly baroque
from the front, from
the side you see that
they are thin tin'*

*(below) Haunting
reminders of camp
life at Bridgend*

roofing felt, covered at the joints with strips of cement sacks. The artist was Mario Ferlito, the youngest man in the camp. In 1993 he returned for the 50th anniversary service, along with a choir from Bologna, when by great good chance his preparatory sketches had just been discovered in the chapel roof. Tears coursed down his cheeks when he saw them again. The candlesticks are the most affecting of all aspects of this little building. Although bulgingly baroque from the front, from the side you can see that they are thin tin – made from twenty-two pound cans of bully beef. What could better symbolize the desire of so many prisoners of war to imagine a better life?

QUIET EVENINGS IN

ᴀʟʟ over the British Isles there are little private palaces in which pleasure can be found – theatres built as tiny architectural treats to tempt you in. King Edward VII arranged one for himself and himself alone – with a single gilded box bulging out on to its little stage – so as to relish the charms of his mistress, the actress Lillie Langtry. It still survives with its original mirrored walls as part of a bar in the Inverness Court Hotel in London – once the home of 'The Jersey Lily'.

In 1901 at Plas Newydd in Wales, the 5th Marquess of Anglesey had the audacity to convert the Gothic fan-vaulted chapel of 1809 into a private theatre. He called it 'The Gaiety' and, having enriched it with plush drapes, quantities of palm trees and statuary, installed a gilded stage in place of the altar. Every performance was to have big stars from London but he himself always insisted on playing the leading role. Laden with jewels – all of them real – he created a fantastical series of outfits – often dressing up as a long-tressed damsel without the slightest attempt to disguise his sleek mustache. Throughout the winter, braziers were lit along the woodland walks of Plas Newydd so that his lissome lordship should never be cold. One day, it is said, they made him too hot and, outraged, he flung his bejewelled fur coat into their flames. Such vanities led him to bankruptcy.

Sir Julian Cahn of Stanford Hall in Leicestershire, who was no less deranged, built a giant Art Deco theatre which, out of terror of Nazi gas attack, he made absolutely airtight! So great was this fear that he designed many escape routes, all progressing through heavy-as-lead submarine doors. One of these dank tunnels still survives, along which you have to scrunch on all fours, on and up through chambers until you reach your goal: one of the finest Art Deco theatres in the land. Frequent air-raid practices were organized in the 1930s in one of which it was said 'Cook, being rather well made, got stuck and set everybody laughing'. She must have been exceedingly well made as the passage is at least three feet wide.

The Cahns enjoyed their Leicestershire and Nottinghamshire evenings (the house is in one county and its park in another) in a number of ways. There were nocturnal swimming parties in their swoopingly 'moderne' pool with the sparsely curvaceous forms of its diving boards streaking through the air. This was built by the chauffeurs, gardeners and grooms. Then there were the four Californian sea-lions: Aqua, Charlie, Freda and Ivy (the last named after two maids in the house) besporting themselves in the parkland pond. Slurping their way through twenty-eight pounds of herring a day, these creatures

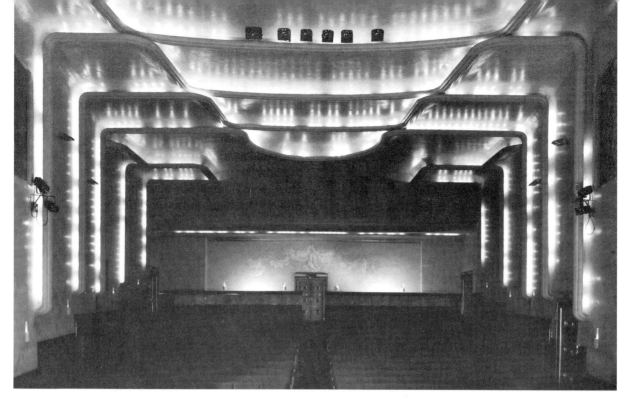

Abracadabra! The nuclear-proof theatre for magic tricks

A masterly 'moderne' pool in Leicestershire

member of the Leicestershire Magic Circle, who had a passion for performing tricks, and it was for these dexterous displays that he built his gargantuan theatre. Some say that he could put on a 'really good show' – he was offered £500 a week to appear at the London Palladium – while others write that his attempts were 'invariably hilarious'. He must have at least looked the dapper dick for the part as he changed his monogrammed silk shirt three times a day every day, and had his hair attended to each morning by a barber – one Sydney Sax – who was given a cottage nearby to be permanently on site.

The theatre was designed by Cecil Aubrey Massey, architect of the great Granada cinema at Tooting. It cost £70,000 to build and, with its complementary architectural lines and lighting, is a superb Art Deco survivor. The murals were painted by Beatrice McDermott 'resting on a sort of celestial

had a pool as well as a house and a see-saw, all prettily placed in the park. There were dozens of flamingoes too, in another fold of the land, not to mention a quantity of pet monkeys.

Sir Julian Cahn was a furniture magnate and a

The jewel of Adelina Patti's country estate

settee' of scaffolding. The American Wurlitzer organ was bought 'slightly second hand' from the Madeleine theatre in Paris.

In 1938 there was a grand spectacular with Sir Julian pulling his best tricks out of the hat. The 'Mental Telepathy Trick' was 'both marvellous and quaint'. With a gramophone on the stage, he would ask members of the audience to whisper the name of their favourite operatic passage. Within seconds the tune would then strike up on the 78rpm record. A wireless transmitter attached to Sir Julian had relayed the request to an assistant who was hidden beneath the boards and who, after a hell-for-leather search among some thousands of records, would play it on a turntable electrically connected to the one on stage! With estate carpenters at the ready, many a device

was designed, such as the 'slimming machine' into which a fat lady stepped, only to emerge as thin as a rake a moment later, and the 'Incredible Disappearing Woman'. Sir Julian had two canaries called Garbo and Sunshine who disappeared and reappeared inside their cage as well as helping Sir Julian with his card tricks. It was said, however, that 'the bowl of disappearing goldfish was a "spectacular" failure but, as the routine was conducted with utmost solemnity, it was irresistibly funny and was always cheered to the echo'.

Another pleasure dome in the home survives most unexpectedly in the Brecon Beacons of Wales. It is an architectural gem of an opera house and theatre, built by the great nineteenth-century operatic diva Adelina Patti, in her grey granite pile, Craig-y-Nos. She had always called it the jewel of her country estate and so it is – a room of pale blue, cream and gold, suddenly

The Marquess of Anglesey, in bankrupting finery –
often as a woman, regardless of his sleek moustache

come upon in bleakly austere surroundings. There are handsome Corinthian columns with gilded capitals marching around the walls and the names of great composers shining forth from the frieze. Patti herself is painted on the safety curtain – thundering along in a chariot in her great role as Rossini's Semiramide. One particularly ingenious device was installed to raise the auditorium floor and the orchestra pit to the height of the stage, thereby creating a sixty-foot-long ballroom.

The opening night on 12 August 1881 was a triumph, with the 'Queen of Song' svelte in her latest Parisian creation – they were mostly hand-made by Worth – welcoming her guests to 'notre petit château de Craig-y-Nos'. She performed Violetta in *La Traviata* and, according to the music critic Herman Klein, had never sung with 'more dazzling brilliancy or greater aplomb. The long-sustained trill on the G–A flat … was as birdlike as ever.' The guests, including Baron and Baroness Julius Reuter (the founder of the news agency), were in ecstasy, standing up from their satin seats and waving their satin

Norman Illingworth, proud as punch of his picturedrome

programmes. The garden scene from *Faust*, next on the bill, was tuned to perfection. 'But the miracle that overshadowed all else,' wrote Klein, 'was the sweet, virginal Marguerite of the singer of forty-eight summers, who could cheat us into the belief that she was still the girl depicted by Goethe … Could this truly be Patti, the inimitable and adorable songstress worshipped in two hemispheres, still looking and still singing like a maid in her teens and striving her hardest to please … down in this remote corner of Wales?'

Life at Craig-y-Nos was luxurious, with both a French and an English kitchen manned by their native chefs. In every room there was a superabundance of rich furniture and fabrics. Contemporary photographs show a jam-packed jumble of objects with such treasures on show as a ruby bracelet from Queen Victoria. Another gift from 'kind friends' was a silver laurel wreath studded with diamonds and engraved with the names of the diva's operatic roles. In the billiard room there was a giant orchestrion – according to Patti the 'soul' of the house – which often accompanied the 'fair châtelaine' as she sang. 'Cookie' the parrot might well have joined in – imitating her 'roulades … further embellished with quite remarkable fioriture of his own'. Adelina Patti lived at Craig-y-Nos for forty-one years and after she died in 1919 almost all the contents of the house were sold. There were decades of grim deterioration but, once again, fully fledged operas are being performed on the stage of Patti's little palace, where the original backdrops still survive. When Verdi was asked who was the greatest singer in the world, he replied, 'La première Patti; la seconde Patti; la troisième Patti.'

Such home entertainment on a grand scale has its modern manifestations. At Ashorne Hall near Warwick, Graham Whitehead has filled his house full of mechanical musical instruments and has built a ballroom on the back of it. Now anyone who wishes to can waltz off to Warwickshire and dance along to the accompaniment of this remarkable collection. The Violina Phonoliszt of 1912 – automatically playing three violins as well as a piano – will move you to tears. The orchestrion with its three-dimensional 'magic picture' of moving trains, windmills, cars and funicular, will make you laugh with delight. Tino the Accordion Boy – life-size with eyes roving and eyebrows rising – will startle you out of your wits. So too will the Blue Angel Robot Organ: a Belgian Art Deco extravaganza with three giant robots playing away on the saxophone, drums and accordion. The ballroom is embellished with decorations salvaged from demolished cinemas nationwide and, when guests drop in, Graham Whitehead has a spectacular surprise in store. With fairy lights flashing and organ chords thundering, up from out of the floor glides the Compton cinema organ of 1933. With its lights changing from one pastel hue to another – it is a rip-roaring relic from the Regal in Hammersmith!

Last but by no means least, for a free evening at the flicks you could do no better than to see Norman and Valerie Illingworth's miraculous transformation of their garage into a little picture palace at Wootton in Bedfordshire. Feeling that the 'night out' glamour of the olden days is dead, they are decked out to greet you. With Norman in a dinner jacket and Valerie in all her usherette's finery, no one can say that home entertainment is dead.

Roving-eyed and eyebrow-raising!

RHUM

SCOTLAND can boast of one of the world's most extraordinary hotels. From the Ritz in Paris to Raffles in Singapore, few can rival Kinloch Castle on the Island of Rhum for the sheer shock of the unexpected. After leaving Mallaig and with four picturesque hours at sea, quaffing away at Irn-Bru, you come upon it – a castellated pile, sitting stately, sheltered and snug in the bay.

Strangely un-Scottish and seemingly plucked from a position of urban civic splendour, it was designed by Leeming and Leeming of London, the architects of the Admiralty and of Leeds Market Hall. It was built in 1901 with pink sandstone boulders, hauled by land and sea from the Isle of Arran, with every one of the workmen being paid an extra shilling a day if they wore kilts on the job.

Sir George Bullough was responsible for these schemes; Kinloch cost him £1 million – the equivalent of some £60 million today – and he was to enjoy it for only two stalking months a year. His fortune was amassed by his father and grandfather in the Lancashire cotton mills, both men having invented a multitude of machine parts, such as the 'Slasher', which set the looms spinning ever more efficiently.

The founder of the firm, James Bullough, wore clogs to his dying day – ever more richly embellished as his fortune flourished. His son George, though, was to become a flamboyant country gentleman and he built Kinloch as a symbol of his aggrandized state. Every inch of its Edwardian opulence is still intact. In 1957 Lady Bullough sold the Island of Rhum, along with the Castle, to the Scottish Nature Conservancy Council – now Scottish Natural Heritage – who have wisely and wonderfully turned Kinloch into a hotel, while leaving it exactly as it was in the Bulloughs' day. Here is a lesson to be learnt: avoid schemes for trim tidiness; do not allow imperfections to be smoothed out by the so often sterile hand of scholarship and prefer the idiosyncrasies of the individual owner over the frequently dead hand of design.

From the moment you open the door, the interior of Kinloch Castle shrieks of the splendour of the age, with the front hall soaring up to double height – smothered with magnificently monstrous Edwardian paraphernalia.

Kinloch is a complete survival of its period. It was decorated throughout in one gluttonous go, with every surface encased in rare woods, silks, satins and velvets. It is filled, for example, with pieces from Shoolbreds, the most favoured furniture store of the day and quite the byword for nineteenth-century luxury. Rarest of all their pieces are the great 'saddleback' sofas and chairs, covered in carpet and dripping with tassels and fringing. Sumptuously swelling and

The Hall – smothered with
magnificently monstrous
Edwardian paraphernalia

as big as baths, to sink into one is to sink into the very bosom of the Edwardian age.

The pulsating heart of Kinloch is to be found, however, under the stairs, with the alarmingly wonderful automatic orchestra – the orchestrion built by Imlof and Mukle. It was ordered by Queen Victoria – who died before it was finished – and was spiritedly snapped up by Sir George and installed at Kinloch. No words can describe the ecstasy of expectation as – with the giant roll hooked on to the works and the single switch pushed down – you wait as it wheezes into life. Suddenly the air is crammed with crashing, loud-as-you-can-listen-to music. The drums beat, the triangles tinkle, the trumpets blow, the pipes play and the bells ring. The castle comes to thrilling life, as if it was singing away to you from under the stairs. Irresistibly compelled to dance, you can prance into the ballroom, with its sofas, curtains and walls of shining yellow silk intact and its frail pod-like silken lampshades still clinging to life. Almost every shade in Kinloch has an Art Nouveau elegance, every one of them a gossamer-fine relic of the turn of the century. For extra luxury in the ballroom there was a balcony for a live orchestra, when the company tired of automatic tones.

In the dining room there is a handsome set of chairs that spent two years going around the world when bolted to the floor of Sir George's yacht, the *Rhouma*. Although their legs were immovable, at a flick of the wrist their great mahogany frames can still spin round for convenience, allowing you to whiz unexpectedly into place at the great Edwardian dining table. You can sit today in the same solid and stately splendour as did the Bulloughs, looking out across the sea to the mainland. You can even gorge on the same delicacies, like venison pie and fresh trout. There has, however, been one change and I am glad of it – that you cannot quaff today as they did at fresh turtle soup, made from tame turtles who lived in a pond on the terrace, keeping company with a host of pet alligators.

The dining room table was an exotic jungle in the early 1900s, with a daily change of dozens of orchids all plunged into bowls of peat. The gardens were magnificent, with a rose garden as well as an Italian garden and lawns stretching down to the sea. Fourteen gardeners worked on them throughout the year. In 1914 they were all called up – they thought as cavalrymen – and, with few of them having ever ridden before, were hoisted on to Highland ponies on the lawn and drilled from dawn to dusk. Few were to return from Flanders.

Life for the rest of the islanders was as spartan as, for those in the castle, it was sumptuous. There were great ornamental-gated kitchen gardens and greenhouses that groaned with such delicacies as grapes and peaches. With the emotional chefs screeching their venison orders in French to the keepers and with the air saturated with scrumptious smells for two months a year, the culinary contrast for the locals must have seemed rough. One of the ghillies' sons wrote of sucking cod's eyeballs 'to assuage our desire for sweetmeats … with careful sucking and manipulation, an eyeball would last all day'. He wrote, too, of how to test whether a 'braxy' infected sheep was fit for consumption: by grabbing it by the hind legs and swinging it six times round your head. If the legs could stand it, you had 'wholesome fairin' . In 1825 the islanders had experienced all the agony of the Highland clearances, with 'the wild cries of the men and the heartbreaking wails of the women and children filling all the air between the mountainous shores'. They are grand mountains and there are many of them and Scottish National Heritage has an excellent programme afoot to preserve the wild eagle in their midst.

Rhum has a single track which forks in two, one bumping off to the laundry – thought to be unsightly to be seen near the house – the other to the great classical mausoleum in Harris Bay that Sir George built for his father, himself and his wife, Monica, who died in 1868. Her coffin was brought up from Newmarket by two elegant top-hatted and tailed undertakers who managed to maintain the dignity of their doleful mission as they were flung about in the Land Rover which carried her on her last journey across the island.

I have what is for me an intriguing connection with Kinloch, in that when my grandmother died – before I was born – my grandfather married the Bulloughs' only child Hermione. 'Grannie', as I always knew her, has died and it is most affecting to see this remarkable place which was so much part of her life.

The castle was the last word in technology. As well as installing the orchestrion, Sir George had an elaborate and early version of double glazing – two panes connected by a folding iron Z. He also installed a fancy telephone with the number 'Rhum 1', as well as a ventilating system arranged in the panelling of the smoking room. Effective and beautiful radiators were built into the hall. Little marble-topped and circular colonnades of heat, they are architecturally distinguished in their own right.

But it is the baths that score the technological bull's-eye at Kinloch: the Shanks patent 'Eureka' – 'The Acme of Luxurious Bathing'. Like a great building in the bathroom, it has an arched wooden cabinet, into which you step for water frolics. Usually there would have been only three variations of aquabatics but the Bulloughs had seven: 'Douche', a dagger-like deluge from above, like an apple corer boring through your head; 'Spray', a delightful embrace of some two hundred needles of water; 'Jet', which consists of ramrods of water up your privates; and 'Sitz', a gentler fountain for the same delicate area; so too is 'Plunge',

but in the form of a flat shelf of water; last of all is 'Wave' – water shooting out of a slit at face level, for as far as six feet if you so desire. The handsome lavatory, a Shanks 'Compactum', is decorated with ferns in deep relief.

Both the Bulloughs' bedrooms are intact. Sleeping in her four-poster, there are few finer views than from Lady Bullough's pillow of the North Sea shoreline. Sir George's bedroom is just as he left it, with the feather-frail tassels and hangings on the bed, his riding boots with their jack by the fireplace and a clock-faced and turkey-carpeted weighing machine. A photograph on the dressing table shows all the comfort of their days on Rhum, with the beautiful Lady Monica casting a fishing line in the harbour, as their great yacht the *Rhouma* lies moored in the background. She made some alarming catches and the house is full of them – six-feet-long pike, strung along the corridors.

The yacht played a large part in their lives: George Bullough was knighted for its work as a hospital ship during the Boer War. She also took the Bulloughs off on a two-year cruise. There are grotesque mementoes from this trip to be found all over Kinloch: a life-size bronze eagle attacking dozens of life-size monkeys, and two hideous Burmese concoctions of urns perched on by eagles and water-spouting dragons standing some twelve feet high. Sir George chose some vividly painted Burmese wrestlers who are viciously locked in combat, and a hauntingly horrible Malay model of a man with ginger hair sprouting from his head, from under his arms and, with particularly vile bristling effect, from around his private parts.

Sir George's holiday snaps, too, are in questionable taste. Handsomely bound in matching albums, they are to be perused at both your pleasure and peril. Intermingled with fascinating views of Sydney and

Hong Kong in their one-horse-town infancies, there are undwellable-on photographs of Chinese executions and punishments.

Every room in Kinloch is still firmly stamped with the character of its Edwardian occupants. The robust smoking room looks through – over a carpeted sofa – to the billiard table beyond where the cues, the scoreboards and the viewing sofa, raised up on a dais, are, of course, all intact. So, too, are – to Sir George's credit – framed testimonials from the Lancashire mill workers. In the hall, where all the Bulloughs gathered, there is still a pencilled note about a goat, written by Sir George to his gamekeeper and a pile of Lady Bullough's songbooks lying on the grand piano.

Stamped with a golden 'Monica' on red calf, they are full of such melodies as 'Wrap Me Up in My Tarpaulin Jacket'. The drawing room is light, bright, white and still sparkling today with all the Edwardian femininity that brought it into being. With candelabras hung with tinkling crystal drops, their candles shaded with embroidered silken ovals, and walls that are hung with rosebud-embroidered silk, it would be difficult to find a more complete reflection of a way of life at the turn of the century. Put 'Ma Blushin' Rosie' on to the orchestrion and finger the frail silk of the drawing room cushions and I defy anyone not to be moved, if only by being able to tune into another time with such precision.

Chinese punishments for photographic pleasure

SOUTHSIDE

HERE are few remaining 'powder closets' in the British Isles like that which has survived at Southside House in Wimbledon. In a room draped heavy with canvas painted as tapestry, there is a hole in the wall, dating from the eighteenth century, into which you poked your head for your wig to be set to rights and repowdered after the winds of Wimbledon Common. A tiny 'Peruke Powder Page' would have done the honours, scrunched into a darkened closet, coiffing away, all the live-long day. There are plenty of such marvels at Southside – a house that is a veritable treasury of British and European history.

It was built in 1687 around the core of a Tudor farmhouse and for the next three hundred years has been infused with a magnitude of startling stories and their attendant souvenirs. A prime example is the pearl necklace that was snatched from the decapitated body of Marie Antoinette on the scaffold. Even more poignant is the attached loop of loosely strung pearls – used by the imprisoned Queen to pay the wardress to allow her a glimpse of her little son, the Dauphin Prince, exercising in the Temple Prison yard below. The necklace was given to a Monsieur Barras who was at the execution as the revolutionary government's representative. He, in turn, gave it to his

mistress Joséphine Beauharnais who, as the Revolution raged, abandoned her lover and struggled to save her family and friends from execution. She turned to the English Embassy for help and a sixteen-year-old youth called John Pennington (from Southside) became the hero of the tale, smuggling out five separate groups of condemned aristocrats from France. Joséphine was, of course, to marry Napoleon and, later, when Pennington was summoned to the Empress to be thanked for his valour, she presented him with the necklace. The Emperor, she said, would not have it in the house: 'Ça non! – Ça non!' For him it was too grim a victor's trophy. And so it lies in Wimbledon today.

Up until the death of my friend Malcolm Munthe – great-great-grandson of John Pennington – in 1995, Southside had been loved and lived in by branches of the Pennington family. His mother Hilda got the story of the necklace from her grandmother whom she could remember very very well, and she was John Pennington's daughter. 'When you come to think of it, there are only two generations between me and the necklace.' Malcolm Munthe was full of such stories – with all minutiae remembered – and spoke with such speed that one was quite overcome by the wonder of his company. Nineteen to the dozen the tales tumbled forth of how, for example, when Henry James came to dinner – which he often did – Malcolm

The comb that tidied the hair on Anne Boleyn's soon-to-be-lost head

had been warned by his father: 'Now don't be surprised, Henry James has to chew every morsel twelve times.' As a result, in Malcolm's words, 'the time, the conversation, the silence became excruciating. We were fascinated, counting – one munch, two munch, three munch, four munch – twelve munches, then he swallowed it.' Malcolm remembered, too, the terror that Hilaire Belloc, the Catholic historian and polemicist, inspired in his childish mind. 'A giant bear of a man with a fierce face and a fur coat to the floor.' Malcolm's father was the Swedish doctor and writer Axel Munthe, whose bestseller *The Story of San Michele* was translated into every language under the

sun. It was to Southside's garden grotto that John Murray, the publisher, would come to discuss the manuscript with its author. Over a hundred years earlier John Murray's great-grandfather – also John Murray – had sat in the same spot, soothed by the trickling water, going over the manuscript of *Childe Harold* with Lord Byron who would ride out to Wimbledon for country air. One of the most moving, though, of all Malcolm Munthe's stories was of scattering his father's ashes off the Swedish coast for which special permission had to be granted by the King – his father's friend and patient. There was a violent storm on the evening they set out onto an ocean of black rollers and the ashes were flung overboard with a sackful of white blossom. That was the last he saw of Axel Munthe – a thousand tiny white flowers rising and falling on the blackened seas.

Southside was deserted only once and then in almost incredibly picturesque circumstances. In 1941, after having been bombed, Hilda Pennington Mellor Munthe was forced to leave, taking what valuables she could to the country. She had no car, but nothing daunted, and with the aid of a local riding master, she hauled an 1830s coach out of the coach house where it had stood for over a hundred years. With no brakes – other than a 'slipper' to be pushed down on to the road before descending a hill by a (non-existent) footman – lined with satin and festooned with crimson 'hammercloth', the 'Berlin' swayed off, out of London at the height of the war on a journey of over 120 miles to Hereford.

Southside is an architectural mix of seventeenth- and eighteenth-century rooms. In the case of the Music Room, one end has its original fireplace dating from the 1680s while at the other stands a fireplace of the mid 1700s. It is a huge room – two knocked into one – that was actually built for a one-day visit of Frederick, Prince of Wales. There is a portrait of Lady

(Temples) One of the most magnificent Masonic temples in the land, that is to be found, of all places, in the Great Eastern Hotel in London's Liverpool Street Station. On the domed ceiling a single star shines – at masonic meetings it is the only light – surrounded by clouds and immense gilded rays in relief. The signs of the zodiac, 'representing the illimitable firmament' sweep round in full circle. With electric flambeaux blazing on bronze tripods the marble walls glow cream 'Skyros Alpha' and red 'Moroccan Onyx', not to mention the black veined pillars of 'Breche violette'.

'The Winged Messengers' – great feathered giantesses 'presenting the light and the dark side of things' in the Watts Chapel at Compton, near Guildford in Surrey. Those of the light have haunting faces gazing out, those of the dark their backs turned: 'Night and Day, Growth and Decay, Ebb and Flow and Joy and Sorrow'. Designed by Mary, wife of G. J. Watts the painter, they are all part of the whirling web of 'Art and Celtic Nouveau' decoration that covers the building both inside and out (Art Nouveau).

Mrs Thatcher (as she then was) sitting as neat as a pin, watching the holy gather to witness Buddha's ascent to preach to his mother – one of the many startling sights to be found on the walls of the 1970s Buddhapadipa Temple in Wimbledon. The scene stretches off to a dream-like collection of buildings: the Eiffel Tower, the Houses of Parliament, as well as the Taj Mahal and, last but by no means least, the Buddhapadipa Temple itself – taking its rightful place in this enchanted architectural landscape (Temples).

above The great Indian Hall at Elveden, built for the Maharajah Duleep Singh between 1863–70. Like a giant living pattern book of Hindu and Islamic architecture, every Moghul style has been represented in this one room (Eastern).

right The Tower Ballroom at Blackpool, designed by Frank Matcham – the king of theatrical design – in 1899. Like a giantess's boudoir upholstered in gold, tiers of boxes bulge forth, swelling on up to the ceiling where a pageant of plasterwork surrounds bewinged and bosomed women as well as paintings of celestial scenes – one with an alarming devil embracing flower-bedecked maidens. Fire reduced this sumptuousness to ashes in 1956, but with inspired grandiosity it was immediately rebuilt to its original design (Fun Days Out).

left The Royal Dairy at Windsor – a bejewelled beauty of a room where a pin could not be pricked between the decorative tiles. The Minton fountain of a mermaid is surrounded by walls of ribbon-entwined oranges and of majolica babies enjoying seasonal pastimes (Glazed Glories).

right The giant head of Typhoeus looms overall in the grotto at Leeds Castle in Kent. Created in the 1980s this sparkling yet sinister underground chamber was inspired by Ovid's *Metamorphoses*: Typhoeus was a terrifying figure who ravaged the earth. The four elements stand as nymphs in niches, all glistening with Bristol diamonds, shells, coral and crystal, flint and blue john. Black and white swans strutt overhead – symbols of Leeds Castle today and of the legendary art of alchemy, said to turn metals into gold (Under the Ground).

One of the most frightening sights to be found in the British Isles: a waxen Sarah Hare glassily staring out of a pedimented cabinet in the Hare Chapel of the Church of the Holy Trinity at Stow Bardolph in Norfolk. All alone save for her marble relations, she has sat here since 1744, when she died from blood poisoning after having pricked her finger whilst Godlessly sewing on Sunday. She is the only surviving waxen funeral effigy in a parish church in the country (Wax).

Hamilton on its walls. She used to come to Southside when she and Lord Nelson lived at Merton House next door, and would perform her 'attitudes' – dressing in the Greek or Roman style and giving 'a living spectacle of masterpieces of the most celebrated artists of antiquity'. It was said, though, that she 'had the ease of a barmaid'. Malcolm's grandmother thought her 'very vulgar'. Goethe, however, praised her performance to the skies. 'It is like nothing you ever saw before in your life.' The platform on which she entranced her audience is still on the floor of Southside's Music Room today. And so too is the table where Lady Hamilton would endlessly play cards – the worse for wear and drink – after Lord Nelson had died.

On one of the occasional tables there is a curious photograph of a lady peering at the camera through her lorgnette. Signed 'Olga 1893' it is the Queen of Greece, born 'Princess of All Russias', and behind this strange little picture lies a tale. John Pennington-Mellor had gone to the Royal Ball in Athens, accompanied by his wife decked out in all the finery of the family jewels – most particularly a great cabochon sapphire in the shape of a fig, set into a double row of diamonds and inscribed, in ancient Arabic, 'God gave me to you! God will keep you for me!' It was one of the rewards given to the Pennington 'Scarlet Pimpernel' from the fleeing French aristocrats. At the Athens ball, suddenly and to her surprise, Mrs Pennington-Mellor found the Queen peering peculiarly closely at the gem. 'You must forgive … when I stare so rudely,' she said. It had reminded her of the legend of a long-lost 'Romanov talisman' but, of course, it could not be the same, she said, 'because ours had inscribed on the back, in old Arabic words, "God gave me…"' Without a word the Pennington-Mellors handed it over. 'No,' said the Queen, 'keep it! Keep it! Lest the luck leaves you as it left us.' She

Reynold's self-portrait and palette; the Queen of Greece and her jewels

must have then posed for the peering photograph and sent it as a souvenir. The jewel still belongs to the family.

Such tales as this can be told with objects throughout Southside, giving one the rarest sense of the particulars of the past. You come suddenly upon a miniature of Charles II along with an emerald that the King gave to his mistress Nell Gwyn. In another corner there is an assembly of objects: a bust, photographs and jewels that all tell a most sorrowful story. The bust is of Hilda Pennington Mellor Munthe, the photographs of Hilda as well as Queen Natalie of Serbia and her son King Alexander, who had unsuccessfully proposed to Hilda. Only a year later his assassinated body was flung to the revolutionary crowds in Belgrade. When the King's mother heard of Hilda's engagement to Axel Munthe she sent the girl – whom her son had loved – mementoes that she had saved.

Then there is Sir Joshua Reynolds's self-portrait, along with his signature, brush and paint-covered palette, that hangs on the walls of the Music Room; while in the dining room you cannot prick a pin between the family and other portraits – painted by masters such as Van Dyck and Burne-Jones. A sword and a tartan plaid hang on high – sad relics of a fatal duel between a Pennington forbear, George Wharton, and the brother of Charles I. Facing them across the room is Philip, 'The Disgusting Duke' of Wharton, created Duke when he was only nineteen years old, who went on to disgrace the family – 'denouncing vice in high places' whilst at the same time plunging into the licentious act-ivities of the Hell Fire Club. According to Pope he was, 'A fool with more of wit than half mankind … Too rash for thought, for action too refined.'

It is the Prince of Wales's bedroom, though, that shines most lustrously of all – a cocoon of

Marie Antoinette's pearls and Charles I's ring

brocades, velvet and sequins that was decorated for the Prince's single visit in 1750. The collection of rarities that belong in here beggars belief. There is, for example, the diamond ring that Charles I took off his finger and gave to Nicholas Kemeys (an ancestor of Malcolm Munthe's) after his valour on the field in the Battle of Naseby. Then there is the exquisite enamel and bejewelled brooch with a pendant death's head and cross that was given to the family again by Charles I as a peace-making token after the duel. Southside is a cabinet of curiosities of improbable rarity. Marie Antoinette's necklace takes centre stage surrounded by such marvels as grass from the field of Culloden as well as a little silver box of congealed cough drops left by Edward VII when he rested here after reviewing manoeuvres on Wimbledon Common.

One of the most heart-stopping of all sights into Southside's past is the portrait of Philadelphia Carey, daughter of Sir William Carey who was married to Anne Boleyn's sister and who accompanied the Queen to the scaffold. This portrait was sent to Queen Elizabeth I so that the Queen could judge her suitability as lady-in-waiting. In her hands, with alarming subterfuge, Philadelphia is holding a comb – the very comb that Anne Boleyn (the Queen's mother) had used to arrange her hair for the descending axe. That comb – unwashed since the scaffold – is still at Southside along with Anne Boleyn's 'vanity box' used on the same sorry day.

TEMPLES

ISHERMEN, Freemasons, the city of Leptis Magna, rotton boroughs, buddhists, what do all these have in common? That temples were built in their honour in the British Isles.

Two monkeys sail romantically out to sea in a shell drawn by dolphins. Watched over by a Cupid monkey – wings fluttering – and holding a wreath of pink roses above their heads, they are serenaded by a fourth member of the happy group, a monkey blowing on a conch. This is just one of the fantastical scenes on the ceiling of a little eighteenth-century fishing temple at Bray in Berkshire. As befits the sporting role of this little building there are also fishing monkeys – one cruelly harpooning a dolphin – and others who are hauling in netfuls of both eels and fish. Two monkey beaters put up a snipe and one, I fear, has shot a kingfisher. Most delicately executed, they are the creations of Andien de Clermont who specialized in 'singeries' – a rococo mannerism of painting monkeys, popular in France and Germany but rare in England. (One other survives also by de Clermont, at Kirtlington in Oxfordshire, where elegant monkeys sit astride greyhounds and hunt the hare.)

The fishing temple at Bray was built in 1744 by the third Duke of Marlborough on an island that owed its existence to the Great Fire of London, when barges carrying stone up the Thames for the rebuilding of the city offloaded unwanted rubble on their return journey to the Berkshire quarries. Thus Monkey Island, as it is now known, became terra firma.

One of the most magnificent Masonic temples in the country is to be found, of all places, in the Great Eastern Hotel at Liverpool Street station. It was built in 1901 by the Masonic directors of the Great Western Railway in a style 'worthy of so important a company and of the serious and dignified purposes of Masonic ceremonial'. Italian craftsmen were brought over and such was the magnitude of marble that the structure of the hotel had to be reinforced to bear its weight. Great studded doors lead you in between two brass pillars surmounted by globes 'which in their detail are pregnant with meaning to the Freemason' – echoing the entrance to King Solomon's Temple. A contemporary account of the opening ceremony described the style of this sombrely glowing room as that 'of the early Greek period, at once elegant, dignified, and noble', with a general effect that is 'restfully solemn'. Such *piano* praise gives scant warning of the riches that encase the room, come upon unexpectedly on the first floor of a London station hotel. With electric flambeaux blazing on bronze tripods, the marble walls shine luminously: cream 'Skyros Alpha' and red 'Morocco Onyx', not to mention the black-veined pillars of 'Breche Violette', their capitals and bases of

bronze. On the domed ceiling overhead shines a single star – during Masonic meetings it is the only light – surrounded by clouds and immense gilded rays in relief. The signs of the Zodiac – 'representing the illimitable firmament' – sweep round the full circle. A golden 'Masonic ladder', 'upon whose rungs are depicted the peculiar symbols of Faith, Hope and Charity', strikes through the sky and, as if in continuation from the 'Sacred Volume' on the Worshipful Master's pedestal, it reaches up to and disappears into the heavens. There is an elaborate organ that 'can be reduced to *pianissimo*, to produce that mystical tone

Monkeys romantically sail out to sea and cruelly kill kingfishers at Bray

which Masons know how to appreciate'. As if this was not enough, there is another temple in the basement of the Great Eastern Hotel, much smaller but in the highly ornate style of ancient Egypt.

Another temple stands by the 120-acre lake at Virginia Water in Surrey – a picturesque assembly of classical columns and carvings that was created in 1750 by 'The Butcher of Culloden', William Augustus, Duke of Cumberland. They have a past

Columns from 600 BC stand proud in twentieth-century Surrey

that is supernatural in its strangeness and, if spirits haunt buildings, it is an exotic bunch that prowl through these pillars in Surrey today. The columns – with separate and elaborate carvings – are arranged as a mock ruined temple. They are fragments of the Roman city of Leptis Magna, which was founded circa 600 BC. A Phoenician city in olive-bearing lands, benefiting from trans-Saharan trade, it became a Roman colony in AD 100 under Trajan. The city flourished during the second, third and fourth centuries when the Emperor Septimus Severus – who was born at Leptis Magna in AD 146 – had ensured its prosperity. There were a host of handsome buildings such as a forum and a basilica, as well as grand colonnaded streets. The splendid solidarity of its surrounding walls saved the city from countless attacks by the Austuriani, but Leptis Magna was to fall finally when destroyed in the fifth century by Gaiseric, King of the Vandals. The ruins were then plundered for hundreds of years – Louis XIV built its statues and columns into Versailles – and in 1816 the Pasha of Tripoli was persuaded by the English Consul-General to make a picturesque present of some fragments to the Prince Regent – soon to be George IV. After the two years of toil involved in hauling them from drifts of white and scorching sand, the great tonnage of granite and marble finally arrived in England where they were offered as a gift to the government. But not the slightest interest was shown in their fate. For another six years the columns, carvings and capitals languished elegantly in the courtyard of the British Museum – no doubt adding immeasurably to the classical look of the place. In 1828 it was George IV who thought up a solution, commissioning Geoffrey Wyatt to enrich his pleasure grounds at Windsor with the treasures. The whole lot was then hauled on great carts – sixteen

A two-headed Gaddafi and Reagan thunder to the aid of Buddha in Wimbledon

horses to a column – from Bloomsbury to Virginia Water. And so pillars that started their lives two thousand years ago (made of stone from ancient Egypt) in the splendour of Phoenician Africa have ended their days in the green belt of Surrey.

Also in Surrey, on a knoll in the grounds of Gatton Park north of Reigate, there stands a little iron-columned Doric temple. It was built as the 'Town Hall' in 1765, to give distinction to the thoroughly undistinguished practice of electing a rotton borough Member to parliament. Gatton, with only a house and church before the Town Hall was built, was just such a borough for 400 years – always with no fewer than two Members of Parliament. One, Sir Thomas Copley aged twenty, was sent to the House in 1554 on the strength of a single vote – his mother's! He was returned with the same handsome majority in 1556, 1557, 1559 and 1563. No fool – Sir Thomas distinguished himself opposing Philip and Mary – he was a zealous Protestant who became a Catholic convert and was imprisoned as a popish recusant. Driven into exile, he was created Baron of Gatton and Master of the Maze by the King of Spain.

The last so-called 'election' to take place at Gatton Town Hall was in 1831 when the Hon. John Saville and J. Ashley-Cooper were returned to the Houses of Parliament. Surrounded by these corrupting columns was the entire force of their constituency: the Duke of St Albans, Colonel Bentinck 'of Nutwood Lodge' and Sir Mark Wood. All of them watched over by a stone urn inscribed with the words: 'When the lots have been drawn, the urn remains. Let the well-being of the people be the supreme law. The place of Gatton 1746. Let evil deception be absent.'

In the Thai Buddhapadipa Temple in Wimbledon, evil is very much in evidence, whipped into a whirlpool of the modern world where Buddha triumphs overall. Ornate and high-pitched gilded gables soar out of the brilliant scarlet and white body of the building, making unexpected companions to their respectable red-brick south London neighbours. Built in the 1970s – the first Buddhist temple in Europe – it was decorated from 1985 with as curious a set of murals as could possibly be conceived. The Bangkok Fine Arts Department, under P. Limprangsi, was responsible for the initial design of the building, with adaptations for northern climes made by Sidney Kaye Firmin and Partners. If the outside dazzles, then the inside will blind. Two Thai artists, Chalermchai Kositpipat and Panya Vijinthanasarn, are responsible for creating the concoction. Over the door Buddha is about to attain the enlightenment, while below him the Evil One, Mara Wasawardi, is on the war-path leading men armed with deadly modern weapons. One fires a machine gun at Buddha whilst a two-headed figure with the faces of Ronald Reagan and Colonel Gaddafi

thunders to his aid. The Earth Goddess Wasunthara weaves to the rescue, squeezing water from her hair to flood the enemy to the edge of the universe. Van Gogh tumbles down in the torrent, about to be struck by a dragon-entwined rocket. An airplane and a boat are on hand to speed you to the Enlightenment. On another wall Buddha preaches his first sermon to the five disciples, surrounded by the charms of the Thai and English landscapes. Other oddities include a painting of Stonehenge, as well as a Henry Moore sculpture and the figure of David Hockney, seated at a table and painting away. The Deputy Prime Minister of Thailand – who arranged for this temple to be built – looks on with his wife, both accom-panied by the King of Thailand. On the south wall heaven is ablaze with celestial beings as Buddha ascends to preach to his mother. The horror of hell churns below while figures from Thai and English life gather between the two. Charlie Chaplin is in the crowd as well as Reg Johnstone who helped the artists – erecting scaffolding, buying paint – with this Herculean task. Most surprising of all, though, is the figure of Mrs Thatcher (as she then was) sitting as neat as a pin, in a navy-blue suit, with her legs crossed and with an Alsatian dog by her side!

The extraordinary scene stretches off into the distance with the most important Buddhist temples and monasteries in the Far East to the left of Buddha, and a dream-like collection of buildings on his right. Perched on little individual mountains of their own are the Eiffel Tower, the Houses of Parliament, the Taj Mahal and, last but by no means least, the Buddhapadipa Temple at Wimbledon, which takes its rightful place in this enchanting architectural landscape.

UNDER THE GROUND

TROLLING down a neat street in the suburbs of Ware in Hertfordshire, you are given no clue to the surprise that awaits you at No. 6 Scotts Road. Trim houses, one after another, suddenly give way to a bulge of trees surrounded by a wooden fence. Peer inside and you see – deep down in a dell – a little classical temple built of flint and stones and embedded and embellished with shells. It is the singular creation of John Scott, a Quaker poet who, yearning for cool climes in the baking hot summer of 1757, built himself a glittering subterranean world.

> O for some secret shady cool recess,
> Some Gothic dome o'erhung with darksome trees,
> Where thick damp walls this raging heat repress,
> Where the long aisle invites the lazy breeze.

He moled his way into the great mound that rises up behind the little building, creating a labyrinth of tunnels, many of them shoulder width and all smothered with stones, flints and shells. Every so often they burst into richly encrusted chambers. In and out, roundabout, and on and on they go, interwoven by tinier tunnels that let in light and air, through which you catch sight of the surrounding woods and sky. When tackling these excavations, Scott wrote that he

had 'marched first, like a pioneer, with his pick-axe in his hand, to encourage his rustic assistants'. He was a man of curious habits who, as often as not, would compose his verses in the dark, then immediately commit them to paper by candlelight. His poems in ragingly romantic rhyme were ornate for a Quaker; indeed his brother, the morbid and melancholy minister, Samuel Scott, persuaded him on his death bed to repent of the frivolities of verse and fancy building.

Doctor Johnson came here in 1773 and wrote that

The 'Fairy Hall' that 'none but a poet could build'

he loved Mr Scott. He described his creation as a 'Fairy Hall' which 'none but a poet could build'. When asked on another occasion whether a grotto would bring welcome relief from the heat, he replied that it would 'for a toad'. The temperature in Scott's grotto at Ware has remained at a steady 48°F since the middle of the 1800s – chilling you to the marrow, rather than cooling soothingly in high summer. There are six chambers, including two 'Committee Rooms' and a 'Coronation Room'. The most sparsely decorated is the 'Robing Room', the walls embellished with sweeping lines of silver ormers and black-knapped flints. It is seventy feet from the entrance – seen through a waist-level, straight-as-a-dye, shell-framed and arched tunnel – into the domed 'Council Chamber' that shines bright with shells, quartz and mica.

Where 'midst thick oaks the subterraneous way
To arch'd grot admits a feeble ray;
Where glossy pebbles pave the varied floors
And rough flint-walls are decked with shells and ores
And silvery pearls spread o'er the roof on high,
Glimmer like faint stars in a twilight sky;
From noon's fierce glare, perhaps, he pleas'd retires,
Indulging musings which the place inspires.

In the 1960s the dome fell in and the grotto was vilely vandalized for years but in 1990 work started on its restoration. Hundreds of shells and minerals, as well as a handsome hoard of Japanese pearl oysters, have been set into the walls with a rich mix of Hertfordshire pudding stone. An interesting detail is that when they restored the grotto, a piece of the Berlin Wall was embedded over the entrance.

Among the many other human moles who have actually lived underground was Robert Watson, Master of the Carlow Hounds in Ireland, who became convinced in later life that he was a fox and built a handsome Gothic-entranced earth for himself in a hill, topping it with a classical temple.

But of all those who have built underground in the British Isles, no one can beat the 5th Duke of Portland for bravado. Between the years 1854 and 1879, he burrowed and built a network of tunnels at Welbeck Abbey in Nottinghamshire – many a hundred yards long – as well as underground stables and pigsties, a railway and, most bizarrely of all, ornamental underground greenhouses (and very fancy and effective they were, too). A man of startlingly reclusive habits, the Duke would communicate to his staff via letter boxes on his door and would venture forth only to offer enthusiastic and knowledgeable encouragement to the thousands of men who were employed in excavating his underground world. Wearing a high hat and a frilled shirt with a stock of fine cambric and with corduroy trousers tied up with a strap around his knees, he was nothing short of loved by his army of a workforce who were, most of them, sure that these vast and totally unnecessary schemes were specifically to give them work in what were then dire times. A Scots workman wrote that he was acknowledged as a brother by 'Portland's noble Duke',

He wastes not all with rich and pride
But keeps the working men employ'd.
… When stocking trade was bad and low
His noble soul for poor did glow.
… Many have the means – but few the will
Their grounds with working men to fill.

One tunnel is 1¼ miles long and wide and high enough to allow two carriages to pass. Whenever he left the estate the Duke would plunge underground through its ornate entrance – the route dipped under the lake, with a tunnel lit by gas – emerging with his carriage's green silk blinds tightly drawn to ensure absolute privacy.

He would shut himself away for days on end, in four or five meagrely furnished rooms – one lined to the ceiling with green boxes filled with brown wigs. Lady Ottoline Morrell came to Welbeck just after the Duke had died – her half-brother had inherited the house – and found all the rest of the rooms to be 'absolutely bare and empty … all painted pink … without furniture except that almost every room had a "convenience" in the corner, quite exposed and not sheltered in any way'. She also wrote of 'the per-

The Duke of Portland's underground ballroom at Welbeck

petual chicken'; a bird would be forever turning on the spit, so that whenever the Duke felt peckish, it would be roasted and ready. Moreover it would be despatched immediately, and at speed, in a heated truck on the underground railway from the kitchens to the house, a distance of some one hundred and fifty yards. Writing of the Duke as a man of 'constitutional shyness' she gave a description of going 'by underground passage and up through a trap door into the riding school'. The roof had been painted as a sunset, the walls were lined with mirrors and crystal chandeliers hung from every corner of the rafters. 'The sudden mood of gaiety that had made him decorate it as a ballroom must have soon faded, leaving the mock sunset to shine on the lonely figure reflected a

Black and white swans, the symbol of Leeds Castle and of alchemy

hundred times in the mirrors around him.' His 'mood of gaiety' had perhaps transferred itself to another colossal ballroom that he was to build underground. Measuring 160 feet by 60 feet, it was also painted pink and lit by mushroom-shaped skylights. 'This feature of Welbeck', wrote a dazzled contemporary, 'is indeed like fairyland in its novelty and in its inward comforts ... the annoyances of wind and of draughts are entirely avoided ... it is a grand conception of its noble owner.' A complex arrangement of hydraulic lifts was built to lower the festive company – which of course never materialized – in their carriages; alternatively, if coming from the house, they could parade down the picture gallery. Statues were to be placed in another gallery through which the guests could stroll between dances. Sadly no statue ever stood in those niches nor was any dance pranced on that floor.

Modern moles are once again in evidence – creating splendours under the sod; none more surprising than the ornamental underpass beneath the Barnstaple and Bideford Road in Devon. Grottos, too, are being undertaken by such artist-craftsmen as

Julian and Isobel Bannerman who, as well as recreating the decorative rockwork underground caves (once used for goats) at Waddesdon in Buckinghamshire, have also built in Oxfordshire a vast 200-metre tunnel clad in blocks of tufa – some the size of a car.

The Italian fashion of the 'Grotta' crossed the seas to the British Isles in the seventeenth century. The Duke of Norfolk was the first to take the plunge, building a tunnel with 'Grot' entrances in 1640 and by the eighteenth century such follies were part and parcel of the stately scene.

As lavish a grotto as has ever been built was created in the 1980s at Leeds Castle in Kent, where your reward for having mastered the mysteries of a maze is to plunge underground into a world inspired by Ovid's *Metamorphosis*, 'where all the creatures of the world suffered changes rich and rare'. The giant head of Typhoeus looms overall – a terrifying figure who ravaged the earth 'issuing from its lower depths' and striking terror into 'heavenly hearts'. Mount Etna eventually sat on his face and as his fierce throat vomited forth cinders and flame, so Mount Etna became a volcano. Water rather than lava 'spews forth' in Kent, churning into this sparkling, sinister chamber. The Four Elements – Air, Fire, Earth and Water – stand as nymphs in niches; all glistening with Bristol diamonds, shells, coral and crystal, flint and blue John. They are protected by mythical creatures of crushed brick. A tradition of grottos is to mix both rich and rubbishy materials together – hence the bones and burnt flint as well as the slag and coal, not to mention saucepans, antlers, skulls and horses' teeth, all giving a sensuous and satisfying texture to the place. Black and white swans strut overhead – the symbols not only of Leeds Castle today but also of the legendary art of alchemy, which is said to turn metals into gold. A life-size white hart is a sorrowful symbol of Richard II, who was imprisoned at the castle on his way to his execution at Pontefract.

Down deeper you delve, surrounded by bones – boiled for days for the job – lining your route to the Styx. This is a world turned on its head; where fishes fly overhead and birds on the floor. An armadillo crawls with its legs in the air and a horse gallops upside down. Hope appears in the form of a phoenix – an enormous bird in mother-of-pearl. The last and most affecting treat is the Rustic Hermitage with its fantastical faces of twisted tree bark and root.

The grotto at Leeds Castle was built as a public attraction and it is a triumph. Would that there could be more. No mere theme park or funfair begins to compare with this fairyland Typhoean's Temple. Why can there not be many more of these glories, rather than the grisly attractions which so many of today's country houses open to the public have sadly come to rely on?

VICARS

THE Church of England has produced battalions of parsons, pastors and prelates of eminence and character: writers, naturalists and inventors, reformers, poets and composers. Cultivated men who were frequently isolated in the country, they were benevolent autocrats of their parishes – in the happy and secure position of being able to pursue their passions unhindered. Other Christian churches – Roman Catholic, Greek and Russian Orthodox – may have produced more profound theologians, more holy saints (and more scandalous sinners, too), more imperious prelates, but none can hold a candle to the Church of England for a collection of incomparably colourful and curious characters.

Prince Pückler-Muskau wrote his observations on the species when he described the hunting parson in his *Tour in England, Ireland and France in the years 1828 and 1829*: 'The most striking thing to German eyes is the sight of the black-coated parson, flying over hedge and ditch. I am told they often go to the church, ready booted and spurred, with the hunting whip in their hands, throw on a surplice, marry, christen or bury, with all conceivable velocity, jump on their horses at the church door, and off – tally-ho! They told me of a famous clerical fox-hunter, who always carried a tame fox in his pocket, that if they did not happen to find one they would be sure of a run. The animal was so well trained that he amused the hounds for a time; and when he was tired of running, took refuge in his inviolable retreat – which was no other than the altar of the Parish Church. There was a hole broken for him in the church wall, and a comfortable bed under the steps. This is right English religion.'

Another such sporting prelate was the Revd Edward Stokes (1706–98) who, although blind, would 'hunt briskly', accompanied by a servant ringing a bell whenever there was a fence to be jumped! Then there was Parson Jack Russell (1796–1883) who first bred the famed terrier and who hunted his own pack at Swymbridge in Devon – despite the vociferous disapproval of his bishop.

While still a student at Oxford he was walking one day 'Horace in hand' on the banks of the Cherwell (according to his curate and biographer the Revd E. W. L. Davies), when 'DIIS ALITER VISUM ...' a milkman met him with a terrier – such an animal as Russell had as yet seen only in his dreams; he halted as Actaeon might have done when he caught sight of Diana disporting in her bath; but, unlike that ill-fated hunter, he never budged from the spot till he had won the prize and secured it for his own.' He called her Trump and she became the progenitress of the famed

Jack Russell terrier. 'It fairly makes a man's heart jump in his waistcoat,' said a local farmer, 'to hear Parsin Russell find his fox; twixt he and the hounds 'tis like a band of music striking up for the dance.' Jack Russell was still in the saddle as well as the pulpit in his old age, 'exuberantly' riding distances of up to seventy miles a day when he was eighty-two years old. Indeed he was on his horse until the end, in that when his three favourite mounts – Billy, Cottager

Parson Jack Russell's reminders of the chase

and Monkey – died, Russell had their 'glossy hides' made into armchairs with 'the legs and hoofs ... beautifully polished and fitted with invisible castors'. Sitting there on his 'faithful brutes ... well might Russell, reclining in the once familiar seat ... be led by fancy's dream to believe that Billy was again under him, sharing the sport together as of yore, and bearing him on eagle-wings to the front of the chase'. Parson Jack Russell left a rich lore of local anecdotes, such as when he found an old lady reading a dictionary by way of diversion. When asked if she was enjoying her

THERE THEY ALL STOOD IN THE DINING ROOM AT TORDOWN, AS IF THE GODS IN A MOMENT OF COMPASSION HAD TRANSFORMED THE TRIO INTO EASY ARM-CHAIRS, DETERMINED THAT RUSSELL AND HIS FRIENDS LIKE BAUCIS AND PHILEMON, SHOULD NOT BE PARTED EVEN BY DEATH.

book she replied, 'Yes … next to me old Bible I do like it best of all, for it doeth explain every word as it goeth on.' Another local figure was the Revd John Froude of Knowstone (a wild moorland parish), known for his 'utter disregard for episcopal authority'. He was summoned by the Bishop but refused to go, so the Bishop went to him. He found Froude sitting by the fire with a flannel over his head and 'with a voice as hoarse as a carrion crow'. Feigning influenza and moaning that he was 'as deaf as a haddock', Froude got rid of the Bishop by the front door while he himself left by the back, put on his 'long gaiters' and went hunting for the rest of the day.

The country vicar was more often than not a naturalist of note – Russell could follow the trail of a fox by sniffing a thistle for its pee. At the same period the Revd William Barker Daniel (1753–1833) delighted the country with his book *Rural Sports* of 1801. It told of such startling practices as tying up a hound bitch in season where a dog fox could serve her. The offspring were 'much esteemed for their handiness in driving cattle; they bite keenly, are extremely active and playful, and are very expert at destroying Weazles, Rats and other vermin'. Despite the sensational success of the book it was said that Daniel 'indulged in sporting tastes to a degree that shocked even his tolerant age'.

Then there was the Revd Pickard-Cambridge (1828–1917) of Bloxworth in Dorset – the 'Father of British Spiders' – who wrote eighty papers on the creatures as well as discovering and preserving 115 different spider specimens. Entomological parsons were no rarity with such figures as the Revd Charles Butler (1560–1647) of Wootton St Lawrence in Hampshire, whose book *The Feminine Monarchie* revealed for the first time that worker bees were female and drones male. He arranged the notes of the bee's song in triple stave so that the reader might hum as the bee hums when swarming. His daughter – his 'sweet honey girl' – was the great-grandmother of the Revd Gilbert White (1720–93), the naturalist, of Selborne whose diaries, along with those of Parson Woodforde (1740–1803) of Weston Longueville and Francis Kilvert (1840–79) of Clyro in Radnorshire, rank among the most endearing accounts of the life of their times. Kilvert wrote of the local schoolmaster learning the violin: 'It had a broken string and there was something wrong with all the rest, and the noise it made fairly raked my bowels … The schoolmaster, however, did not appear to notice that anything was wrong. His wife held the book up before him. "Glory be to Jesus," sang the schoolmaster, loudly and cheerfully sawing away the cracked and broken strings … shriek, shriek, scream, groan, yell, howled the violin … and still the schoolmaster sawed away vigorously and sung amid the wailing, screeching uproar, "Glory be to Jesus" in a loud and cheerful voice. It was the most ludicrous thing. I was never so hard put to it not to laugh out loud.'

Some clergymen had country life forced upon them, like the great wit Sydney Smith (1771–1845), who was despatched from the salons of London to Foston in Yorkshire and thence to Combe Florey in Somerset. 'Had England a hierarchy formed of all wits,' wrote Thomas Moore, 'whom but Sydney would England proclaim as its primate?' It was said that Sarah Siddons, who never jeopardized her deportment as a tragedy queen by lapsing into laughter in society, fell an easy prey to Sydney Smith's humour at their first meeting, developed convulsions, and had to be helped from the table. He was famed for his turns of phrase, the most famous being 'a square peg in a round hole'. (He said, in fact, that in life a square person would be sure to 'squeeze' himself into a round hole.) His definition of marriage goes: 'It resembles a pair of shears, so joined that they cannot be separated, often moving in opposite directions, yet always punishing anyone who comes between them.' From thousands more one or two will have to do: 'My whole life has passed like a razor – in hot water or in a scrape'; 'The heat was so dreadful that I found there was nothing left for it but to take off my flesh and sit in my bones'; to his brother: 'You and I are exceptions to the laws of nature. You have risen by your gravity, and I have sunk by my levity.' In London he shone in the company of Byron,

The 'Queen of Science' dances through The Water Babies

Talleyrand and Sheridan and in the country (which he saw as a 'healthy grave') he kept his spirits afloat by teasing the local squires. For example, when dining out at the parsonage of a neighbouring church where he was to deliver the sermon, he sent a Mr Kershaw into near fits of apoplexy. 'You must not laugh at my sermon tomorrow,' said Smith, to which the shocked squire replied that he hoped he knew the difference 'between here and church'. Smith bet Kershaw a guinea that he would make him laugh and the next day interrupted his sermon with a succession of 'sneezes' exploding the word 'Ker-shaw' over and over again from the pulpit. A guffaw burst from the squire, the congregation and the parson were scandalized and Smith won his bet. He also took particular pride in doing the work of the 'graduated homicides' as he called doctors. He invented a 'patent armour for rheumatism' – large 'jack boot' buckets for the legs, leg-of-mutton-like contrivances for the shoulders and a helmet for the head, all of tin, to be filled with hot water when in use. Smith was made Canon of St Paul's in 1831 and when Queen Victoria visited the City to open the Royal Exchange he was put in charge of the arrangements – to the irritation of the city companies. 'Perhaps Mr Smith these details are better left to us? Too many cooks, you know, spoil the broth.' 'Very true, Sir,' replied Sydney Smith, 'but let me set you right in one particular. Here there is but one cook – myself. You are only scullions, and will be good enough to take your directions from me.'

Charles Kingsley (1819–75) was another giant in this field already peopled by armies of colossi. Starting to write both poems and sermons when he was only four years old, he took orders in 1842 and thereafter became a great social reformer as well as an educationalist, an amateur scientist and a theologian, not forgetting a writer of poetry and prose. His most magical book *The Water Babies* was the only one,

the Sangraal'. He built his vicarage at Morwenstow in Cornwall, designing five of its chimneys as models of the church towers where he had held previous livings. 'The sixth,' he wrote, 'perplexed me very much, till I bethought me of my mother's tomb; and there it is, in its exact shape and dimensions.' Seeing himself as 'a fisher of men', Hawker dressed accordingly, with a blue fisherman's jersey (knitted with a red cross to mark the wound of the centurion's spear), a claret-coloured tail coat, hessian boots to the knees, with either a 'Wide-awake Beaver' or a pink fez on his head. 'I do not,' he said, 'make myself look like a waiter out-of-place.' He wrote that 'The Animals were the Attributes of God visibly roaming the Earth' and most picturesquely practised what he preached, appearing daily at his lectern – often with no congregation – attended by up to nine cats and his dog. According to a writer in the *Standard* these were 'unusual but graceful acolytes who, as he assured us, allowing for an occasional display of youthful vivacity, rarely conducted themselves otherwise than with great propriety'. He even went so far as to have a pet pig 'of the Berkshire breed, well cared for, washed and currycombed, which ran beside him whenever he went for walks and paid visits'. Even into ladies' drawing rooms for tea. If this proved unpopular, off the black creature would slink, its tail 'distinctly out of curl'. Animals, he said, were more fitting than many Christians 'within the ark' of his church. He was convinced of the underlying unity of creation.

The issue of whether animals have souls taxed the nineteenth-century clergyman. The Revd Augustus Toplady (1740–78) – author of the hymn 'Rock of Ages' – declared that he firmly believed that beasts have souls, 'souls truly and properly so called'. An

according to his wife, that he wrote 'with real ease'.

The Revd Stephen Hawker (1803–75) was also a writer of distinction – a poet-parson, held in high esteem by Tennyson, who admitted that he had 'beaten me on my own ground … with his Quest for unnamed 'Divine' thought otherwise and would allow vermin to bite him without hindrance: 'We shall have Heaven to reward us for all our sufferings, but these poor creatures have nothing but the enjoyment of the present life.' The Revd J.G. Wood (1827–89), who invented blinkers for horses, wrote over sixty books on animals, including hefty volumes on their immortality entitled *Man and Beast: Here and Hereafter.* He had many letters of abuse including one from a correspondent who said that 'he would never condescend to share immortality with a cheese-mite. I replied that he would be consulted on the subject; and that, in the second place as he did condescend to share mortality with a good many cheese-mites, there would be no great harm in his extending his conde-scension a step further.'

The roll call of colourful clergy is long.

JOHN SKELTON (1460–1529) Diss, Norfolk. First Poet Laureate.

WILLIAM LEE (died circa 1610) Calverton, Nottinghamshire. Inventor of the stocking frame.

ROBERT HERRICK (1591–1674) Dean Prior, Devon. Poet, wrote of congregation as 'a people currish, churlish as the seas, and rude amongst the rudest savages'.

STEPHEN HALES (1677–1761) Teddington, Middlesex. Scientist, botanist, physiologist. Inventor of an artificial ventilator applied to pris-ons and ships.

LAURENCE STERNE (1713–68) Sutton-on-the-Forest, Yorkshire. Author of *Tristram Shandy*.

GEORGE CRABBE (1754–1832) Muston, Leicestershire. Eminent poet. Set on his feet by Burke, Jane Austen said 'she could fancy being Mrs Crabbe'.

WILLIAM KIRKBY (1759–1850) Barham, Suffolk. Entomologist, collected 153 species of bees.

THOMAS ROBERT MALTHUS (1760–1834). Pointed out the inevitability of population control but produced children himself.

RICHARD HARRIS BARHAM (1788–1845) Snargate, Kent. Author of *Ingoldsby Legends*.

HENRY LYTE (1793–1847) Lower Brixham, Devon. Author of 'Abide With Me' and 'Praise My Soul the King of Heaven'.

HENRY MOULE (1801–80) Fordington, Dorset. Inventor of the earth closet.

SABINE BARING-GOULD (1834–1924) Lew Trenchard, Devon. Author of 'Onward, Christian Soldiers' as well as 159 books.

FRANCIS ROSSLYN COURTENAY BRUCE (1871–1956) Herstmonceux, Sussex. Bred green mice.

HAROLD DAVIDSON (1876–1937) Stiffkey, Norfolk. 'The Prostitutes' Padre', defrocked, ended life on show in a lion's cage.

WILLIAM KEEBLE MARTIN (1877–1969) Coffinswell and Milber, Devon. Naturalist with sensational success, aged eighty-seven, of *Concise British Flora*.

WILBERT VERE AUDRY (b. 1911) Emneth, Norfolk. Author of the *Thomas the Tank Engine* books.

CHAD VARAH (b. 1911). Founder of the Samaritans.

MARCUS MORRIS (1915–1989). Founder of *Eagle* and *Girl* comics.

Strangest and saddest of all is the tale of the Revd George Garrett (1852–1902), curate of Moss Side in Manchester. He invented the mechanically powered submarine, the RESURGAM – 'I shall arise', which was launched in 1879, after having been pulled by thirty shire horses to the Great Float off Birkenhead. No sooner launched, however, than the iron fish sank in Colwyn Bay. The brave curate managed to escape and, in time, offered his invention to the navy of the

Ottoman Empire, where their admirals, being of a
more trusting nature than the Lords of the British
Admiralty, gave him and his machine a second chance
– to equally little avail. After vicissitudes galore in the
international arms trade, including a long association
with the most notorious arms dealer of all – Zaharov –
he ended life as a destitute out-of-work fireman in
New York, never knowing of the part his invention would play in the eventual development of
the modern submarine.

From Sydney Smith to Marcus Morris, all
these men of the cloth have managed, while
fulfilling their religious duties, to contribute
more to the gaiety of the nation than ten thousand fops and dandies.

'As the French say,' wrote Sydney Smith,
'there are three sexes – men, women and
clergymen.'

Eagle *comic, the creation of a clergyman*

WAX

I N 1711 a waxen Margaret, Countess of Heningbergh – 'Lying on a Bed of State, with her Three hundred and Sixty-Five Children, all born at one Birth, and Baptised by the names Johns and Elizabeths' – was exhibited by a Mrs Salmon in Fleet Street. The Countess, with her 'miraculous *accouchement*', had a merry band of companions, all made of wax, many of whom moved: 'Hermonia a Roman Lady, whose father offended the Emperor, was sentenced to be starved to Death, but was preserved by Sucking his Daughter's breast'. Then there were 'the Canaanitish Ladies, Offering up their First-born Infants, in Sacrifice to that ugly Idol, [Moloch] in whose Belly was burning a Furnace to destroy those Unhappy Children'. They were described as 'All richly dress'd and composed with so much variety of Invention, that it is wonderfully Diverting to all Lovers of Art and Ingenuity'. When you had had your fill of Mrs Salmon's show, a waxen and mechanized 'Mother Shipton' kicked you out through the door.

Such exhibitions were popular from the mid-1600s when simple booths in the street would display waxworks for diversion. From the 1680s onwards there were ever more elaborate tableaux to tempt in the crowds, culminating in the palatial premises of the champion of all wax modellers Madame Tussaud, which opened in London in the 1830s when she was seventy-five years old. 'Nothing seems wanting, but life and motion' was the clarion call of the waxwork exhibitors. After Mrs Salmon's death in 1760, her establishment survived well into the 1800s with such spectacles as 'Shepherds and shepherdesses, with lambs and a goat or two, making violent love, in a mode scarcely proper to … polite notions'. In 1818, at Savile House in Leicester Square, there was a tableau of the utmost morbidity. In a room draped in black, beneath a canopied bier and surrounded by candles, lay the twenty-one-year-old Princess Charlotte, who had died the year before in childbirth. Her stillborn baby lay by her side.

Marie Tussaud (née Grosholtz) opened in London in 1835. She had started modelling in wax in France when she was six years old, under the guidance of her uncle Johann Wilhelm Christophe Curtius, whose 'Cabinet de Cire' was famed throughout Paris. Voltaire sat for Marie when she was only seventeen and, two years later, she moved into Versailles, having been appointed as art tutor to Madame Elizabeth, sister of Louis XVI. As the revolution rumbled, so the lives of Marie and her uncle became ever more sinister – tiptoeing along the tightrope of the troubles. Never putting a foot wrong, they befriended revolutionaries, royalty and grandees alike. Suavely socializing during one week, they could find themselves smoothing out the skin of those same friends' severed heads the next. Marie, still in her twenties, must have found it particularly gruesome to cradle the blood-slippery face of the King's sister for whom she had worked for six years.

After a failed marriage, Madame Tussaud moved to England. Mrs Salmon's established waxworks beat her at her own game and she set off on a tour around the British Isles, which was to last for thirty-three years, ending only when she was seventy-four years old. She set up permanent premises in Baker Street, founding an attraction that has now been flourishing for 160 years. The illustrious were honoured in superior surroundings. 'The Corinthian Saloon' alone was lit by 500 gas jets and they were reflected a hundred-fold in mirrors. With such extravagances as the purchase of George IV's coronation robes for £18,000 they trounced all competitors.

You paraded through the midst of the models to the strains of an orchestra and lounged on fringed ottomans to enjoy the show. The Duke of Wellington was a constant visitor, coming alone before Madame Tussaud's opened to stare long and hard at Napoleon on his funeral bier.

Today, when their popularity dims, many of the models are changed, and their heads despatched to Wookey Hole in Somerset. A precious few have found their way into private hands.

The notorious body snatchers Burke and Hare have been on display since the opening of Madame Tussaud's. (There is a wallet believed to be made out of Burke's skin in the Royal College of Surgeons in Edinburgh.) Their illicit activities had popularized the 'Anatomical Waxwork' and many a startling 'flayed' exhibit was crafted for public enjoyment.

Rackstrow's Museum of Anatomy and Curiosities was another London attraction, 'with more detail … than would be considered desirable in a public show'.

Scrawny-breasted Age at the Wallace Collection

There was a model of a woman, complete with glass veins, filled with 'liquors resembling the arterial and veinous blood', coursing through her waxen body, as well as machinery making 'the action of the heart and motion of the lungs in breathing'. The 'Anatomical Venus' shown off by Dr Joseph Kahn was also a popular draw which could be dismantled into eighty-five pieces. 'Gentlemen Only' was often the sinister sign to be seen outside such showroom doors.

Anatomical waxworks had their beginnings in France and Italy in the seventeenth century and were in full and grimly beautiful flower during the 1700s and 1800s. Many hospital museums in Britain have such fully 'flayed' waxen men and women.

Gaetano Zumbo was the great modeller in Italy during the late 1600s. He is credited with being the first to use paint on wax and his representation of a plague-afflicted head – riddled through with worms – in Lo Specolo Museum in Florence is a sight never to be forgotten. The Victoria and Albert Museum has a few of Zumbo's wax tableaux: another way of working with wax producing framed pictures in the medium that were all the richer for being three dimensional. It began at the end of the sixteenth century and Zumbo's *Time and Death* shows a ruinous vault in an architecturally rich cemetery. The naked figure of Time, scythe at the ready, points to a clock as all around him bodies decompose. Snakes writhe, and rats – their fangs bared – run through the ruins. A live beggar sits grinning and a crowned skeleton waves a sceptre over all. The Marquis de Sade greatly admired Zumbo's works and wrote of them in *Juliette:* 'So powerful is the impression produced that even as you gaze at it your other senses are played upon, moans seem audible and you wrinkle your nose, quite as if you could detect the evil odours of mortality.'

These minute statuary were also wrought to a fine pitch with little portraits that were being made as early as the fifteenth century in Italy. Both Michelangelo and Benvenuto Cellini applied themselves to the medium. In 1550 Vasari wrote, 'It would take too long to enumerate all the artists who model wax portraits, for nowadays there is scarcely a jeweller who does not occupy himself with the work.' Real jewels as well as real hair were frequently used on these exquisite and often painted representations, sallying forth from the flames. They were the works of the sculptor, jeweller and painter, all in one. 'Youth and Age' was a favourite theme, with two semi-nude

portraits, one a beauty with bosoms bulging, the other a grotesque with scrawny breasts. The Victoria and Albert Museum and the Wallace Collection both have examples, dating from the seventeenth century. In Britain the wax portrait was popular throughout the eighteenth and nineteenth centuries with such sculptors as John Flaxman mastering the medium.

Wax modelling as a funeral art was practised as early as 300 BC when the Greeks and Romans would have coloured images made of the deceased. After the funeral the bust or head would be placed in a wooden cupboard in the atrium of the home. In Britain, the first recorded waxen funeral effigy was for General Monck, Duke of Albemarle, in 1670. His head and hands were of wax and his armoured body of sticks and straw. It was ordered for his funeral by Charles II as an improvement on the hitherto wooden images that had lain in processional state upon the coffins. (They, in turn, had replaced the corpse itself after the tardy funeral of the murdered Edward II had made that tradition untenable.) Charles II was to have no funeral effigy at all but, instead, a fine wax model was later made of him – again only the head and hands with a stuffed body of wood and iron – showing him, in Marvell's words: 'of a tall stature and of sable hue'. His lofty figure 'above two yards high' stands with the rest of the great collection of wax and wooden kings, queens and dignitaries at Westminster Abbey. There are ten richly clothed waxen funeral effigies with only one recumbent figure, the young Edmund, Duke of Buckingham, who died aged nineteen from consumption and was the last to be lain on a coffin. All the rest of the models in the Abbey, standing life-size and life-like, must have made alarming guests at their own funerals.

The last effigy in the land to do so was the refined form of Frances, Duchess of Richmond, modelled by a Mrs Goldsmith. The Duchess was known as 'La

Zumbo's Time and Death

Belle Stuart' and Pepys lay awake all one night, his mind lingering on her 'sweet eye, her little Roman nose and excellent *taille*' and imagining 'sport' with her 'with great pleasure'. At Westminster, her beauty preserved – she was to be disfigured by smallpox – she still keeps company with the parrot she had loved and lived with for forty years. Three wax figures were added to the Abbey collection just for show in the eighteenth and nineteenth centuries: first, Queen Elizabeth whose wooden effigy had rotted; second, William Pitt, Earl of Chatham, who was buried at

Westminster 'near the dust of Kings'; and third, Lord Nelson, who was installed in 1806. The likenesses of both statesman and Admiral were said to be startling. Nelson was modelled by Catherine Andras, who exhibited her waxworks at the Royal Academy; Pitt's was produced – from life – by Patience Wright, a highly successful American wax artist who was reputedly a spy for Benjamin Franklin during the American War of Independence. Although calling the King and Queen 'George' and 'Charlotte' and on friendly and business terms with London's illuminati, she was thought by some to be 'the Queen of Sluts'. It is sad, indeed, that only Pitt's face survives, showing the eerie brilliance of her work. During the Second World War all the Abbey's waxworks were safely stored in Piccadilly Circus Underground Station.

Only one other splendidly attired funerary effigy in wax survives in the country, and a great and terrifying surprise it is to come upon. It is of Sarah Hare, whose effigy has stood, glassily staring, in a little pedimented cabinet – all alone save for her marble relations – in the Hare Chapel of the Church of the Holy Trinity at Stow Bardolph in Norfolk. My ex-mother-in-law Whilhelmine Harrod was the first to rediscover her in 1955. 'One wet Autumn evening, just before dusk, I looked into a church at Stow Bardolph, on the edge of the Fens … my guide book referred in a discouraging way to "the poor 16th century Hare chapel". Knowing that guide books are made to be disagreed with I went ahead.' After seeing the splendour of the monuments and reading their inscriptions, she 'was about to leave in a rather melancholy frame of mind, when I noticed in a corner of the chapel a fine mahogany cupboard with a pediment and an inscription. I do not know what I expected to find because in the dim light I did not read the lettering, but with only the slightest degree of apprehension I opened the cupboard door. Here indeed was a subject for Dr James [the great ghost story writer M.R. James]. Peering at me, her eyes glistening, the hands and bosom appearing to move in the shadows, sad, distraught, with a mottled face, dressed in a white tucked silk gown, with a red cape and hood over her ringlets, upright in a box, stood a young lady dead for over two hundred years. I was frightened, really frightened. I was alone in the church; outside the rain was beating down and leaves were being blown against the windows … I am glad to say that I was brave; I turned on the lights and read that Sarah Hare, dying in 1744, had directed that her effigy, in wax,

should be kept in that place.' She had died from blood poisoning, having pricked her finger whilst Godlessly sewing on a Sunday. Her will was a detailed demand for an unostentatious funeral – 'to be buried in one of my own blankets in place of a burial dress' and that the coffin should not have 'any ornament that is not absolutely necessary'. She was to be conveyed to church in the 'cheapest method possible', either cart or wagon. 'They that humble themselves shall be Exalted.' It would seem therefore that this remarkable effigy was an exercise in scholarship rather than self-importance – following the customs of ancient Greece and Rome rather than the exalted traditions of royalty. The funeral art of waxen images was brought back to its original purpose in a Norfolk parish church.

A wax figure of quite a different order sits in a cabinet in University College, London – an 'Auto-Icon', a man whose image has been preserved for the benefit of humanity. It is Jeremy Bentham, the great philosopher and law reformer who was determined to show that the dead could be put to good use for the living. He left his body to his friend Dr Southwood Smith with the instructions that it be used as 'the means of illustrating a series of lectures to which scientific and literary men are invited … first to communicate curious and highly important knowledge and secondly to show that the primitive horror of dissection originates in ignorance … and that the human body when dissected instead of being an object of disgust is as much more beautiful than any other piece of mechanism as it is more curious and wonderful.' His wishes were carried out, with Dr Southwood Smith delivering the lecture at the Royal College of Physicians – during a violent thunderstorm – 'with a clear and unfaltering voice, but with a face as white as that of the dead philosopher before him'. Bentham's head was to be preserved untouched. By 'placing it under an air pump over sulphuric acid [it] was rendered as hard as the skulls of New Zealanders; but all expression was of course gone'. (Bentham and his friend had already experimented in this regard by slowly drying a human head in an oven at Bentham's house.) A wax model was, therefore, made by 'the distinguished French artist' Jacques Talrich, who also presumably made the hands. All, according to Southwood Smith, 'a most admirable likeness'. Bentham's will decreed that his friend should put his skeleton together 'in such a manner as that the whole figure may be seated in a chair usually occupied by me … in an attitude in which I am sitting when engaged in thought in the course of time employed in writing'. It was to be clad in one of his black suits, with his 'staff' which he called 'Dapple' in his hand. Bentham also suggested that his figure should join any gathering of his 'personal friends and other Disciples should [they] be disposed to meet together … for the purpose of commemorating the Founder of the great happiness system of morals and legislation'. In his work on the 'Auto-Icon, or the Uses of the Dead to the Living' written between 1831 and 1832, he declared that every man, if embalmed, might be his own statue. 'If a country Gentleman has rows of trees leading to his dwelling, the auto-icons of his family might alternate with the trees; copal varnish would protect the face from the effects of rain – caoutchouc the habiliments.'

Such schemes, though, were not for him; after seven years of sitting in a cabinet in his 'dear friend' Dr Southwood Smith's house, Bentham's effigy was given to University College – he was the inspiration behind its founding – where it has remained to this day. His head is kept in a most elegantly designed separate box.

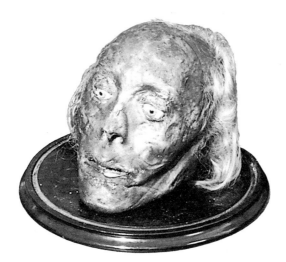

Jeremy Bentham's dried head

XANADU

STOKESAY Court in Shropshire has had a peculiarly poignant past. It was built in the late 1880s for John Derby Allcroft, who founded his fortune on the realization that every church-going lady – however poor – needed a pair of gloves for Sundays. He manu-factured white cotton gloves by the thousand. They were cheap, they fell apart, they had to be renewed, and so the fortune was made – money that was to be poured into possessions and into the building of Stokesay, a sure symbol of his new-found status. In 1939, at the onset of the Second World War, almost all its contents were packed away into an acre of attic, where they remained – despite the house being lived in – for another fifty-five years. On the death of Allcroft's granddaughter, the treasures were rediscovered in all their unruined richness. The house was reinstated to its original state for three magical weeks and then the whole bang lot sold off in a three-day sale.

Building Stokesay had cost the equivalent of some £20 million. The arched and balustraded double-height hall was enriched with a wealth of woodwork, all made at Baltic Wharf in London and hauled up to Shropshire by train. One wall had to be strengthened to hold a life-size marble sculpture of the Allcroft boys, Herbert, John, Walter and Arthur, with their pet rabbits, chickens, dogs and doves. As this was being carved in the studio Mrs Allcroft was apparently so delighted with their likenesses that 'she used enthusiastically to kiss the little marble faces as they emerged from the stone'.

Stokesay was technologically up-to-the-minute. In the hall, the elaborately carved pillars conceal down-pipes. Air was sucked along tunnels under the house, and up across heated metal plates beneath the stairs. (The plates were kept hot by a *Queen-Mary*-sized boiler in the basement.) It was one of the first houses in the British Isles to have electricity and there were countless bare bulbs blazing in all their innovative glory. Even more celebratory were the pendants for the dining room ceiling which were actually designed to look like light switches. Globes glowed on the gateposts, when there was barely running water in most of the homes nearby.

Thomas Harris was the architect who, strange to say, is credited with being the first to use the term 'Victorian architecture'. At Stokesay he produced a suitably solid 'Jacobean' pile for his client, but with an exterior and an interior that was lumpen rather than lovely. It was built in four main blocks – all 'zoned' with propriety. The central and main rooms acted as a bulwark between the 'Ladies' Wing' and the 'Gentlemen's Wing' built for the Allcroft sons as well as visiting bachelors and their valets. The servants had a wing of their own with rooms as narrow as coffins.

John Derby Allcroft died only a year after he had moved in, and the house was inherited by his son Herbert – an inveterate traveller who, seeing the world as a giant emporium, had exotica shipped back to Shropshire by the ton. He snapped up miniature porcupine furniture from America and despatched two sets of armour – dating from the sixteenth and seventeenth centuries – from Japan. He bought quantities of objects from 'Mr Beaton's curio store' in Mandalay in 1895, where he even managed to get his hands on to King Thebaw's chair looted from the Golden Palace. (In Calcutta, the Great Eastern Hotel was so booked up that he was forced to sleep in a tent on the roof.) So great was the number of crates that some were never even opened – one in the attic was found to be full of 300 palm leaf fans.

Herbert had married a grandee, Cissy Russell, who brought a host of heirlooms to the house, so what with these and the frenzied fruits of her husband's shopping, together they stuffed Stokesay to the brim.

Brigadier Johnny Rotton

When Herbert died, Cissie Allcroft married again – to Brigadier Johnny Rotton. It was she who packed all the contents of the house into the attics during the war. When she died, Stokesay was inherited by her daughter Jewell (pronounced Jew-elle) who, in the post-war years of austerity, felt no desire to unpack the treasures again. She was to live on at Stokesay with her husband Sir Phillip Magnus, the historian and biographer, in the rattlingly empty rooms – save for one or two downstairs none was refurnished. In the drawing room, which was one of the few that they occupied, the drawers were jam-packed with her and her mother's letters and Brig. Johnny Rotton's photograph – in upright military splendour – was drawing-pinned on to a velvet panel on the walls. It was here that you could compare the fate of the furniture which had been used to that which had been stored in the darkened attic. For example, a set of crimson silk upholstered chairs in the drawing room are faded to greyish pink and in shreds and tatters, making sad companions for their sheeny ruby red sisters, who had spent their lives upstairs in the dark. These were made by Howard and Sons who, incidentally, also fitted out the Vanderbilts' yacht.

After her husband's death, Lady Magnus lived on alone in Stokesay, in the far-off 'Ladies' Wing', refusing to come downstairs and refusing even to look out of the window. When she died in 1992 the attic doors were opened, shedding the first light of day for fifty-three years on the treasures that had been trapped in the top of the house. There were hundreds of every-day objects too, such as coal scuttles, lamps, fireguards and fire irons as well as a multitude of mugs. Cushions and curtains emerged in their original brilliant hues, and there were silken ropes and tassels by the score. The Army and Navy Stores had once supplied large wooden boxes of bars of carbolic soap – each one incised into daily rations for the maids – and they were all still there in the attic. Fortnum & Mason had provided a large lump of grey 'Selected Sun Dried Turtle' which survived, along with a later letter apologizing for not having included instructions for making turtle soup. When simmered for nine hours the grey mass was promised to swell four-fold. Then there was a cheroot holder given by the German Emperor to Herbert Allcroft, as well as an opium pipe which he had smoked in Hong Kong – 'not very nice and made me feel rather stupid'. This after dining at a 'swell restaurant' with 'a band that made the most hideous noise all the time', as they got their choppers into sharks' fin, fishes' maw and sea slugs.

Herbert's bedroom at Stokesay, shut up after his death in 1911, was discovered to have a medicine cupboard still intact with such tonics as 'Le Plus Radioactif de France' – Life Enhancing Radioactive Water! A mass of military mementoes was uncovered too – dashing plumed hats in tin boxes. One, a 'Bell Topped Shako', belonged to Herbert Allcroft's father-in-law, General Sir William Russell, a hero of the Crimea and Lucknow. Then there was his flag taken from the mutineers at the Siege.

The history of the house has been strange indeed. It had a fully fledged life for just twenty-one years, a half-life for another twenty-six and, thereafter, fifty-five years of obscurity, packed away from itself in its own attic. Sotheby's gave Stokesay its final swan song in September 1994. Under the sympathetic and neighbourly guidance of Robert Holden, who had been the first to open the attic doors, and with the aid of a complete set of photographs that had been taken of Stokesay in its heyday, the house was brought back to life for a last huzzah. It was stripped bare and this time for good, within only three days. Now only the four marble boys remain – they were built into the walls so they can never leave. They are all alone in the house that their father built, with dreams of eternal splendour, a little over a hundred years ago.

Y Oh Why?

S⸿ Bartholomew's Hospital is doomed to die an inglorious death, after nearly a thousand years of inspirational leadership in the history of medicine. It is the oldest and greatest hospital in the country and one of the three most venerable in the world, with only Santo Spirito in Rome and the Hôtel-Dieu in Paris playing equally heroic roles in the hospital evolution of the Western world. Unless a miraculous scheme is devised – and there are battles raging for Barts – two twentieth-century politicians, Virginia Bottomley and Stephen Dorrell, will be responsible for crushing the very cradle of medicine in the British Isles, succeeding where other more tremendous forces have failed. Barts has, in its history, defeated not only the plague and the dissolution of the monasteries – it was started as a religious institution – but also the Great Fire and, more recently, the encircling flames of the two World Wars when its very walls were pitted and warmed by the blitz.

This great institution has been famed for centuries and its up-to-the-minute modernizations are as innovative today – with its new £15 million John Abernethy Suite which has the most technically advanced operating theatres outside America – as they were in 1123, when it was founded as a sanctuary for the ill, the aged and the passing stranger. In those days foundlings and orphans were plucked from the gutter in such droves that it was deemed suitable to employ a Latin master for their benefit.

Ever since these early beginnings St Bartholomew's has been acknowledged as a great monument to medicine. Far less well known is that over its 873-year history the hospital has amassed a vast archive collection, as well as an assembly of objects and of art and architecture that is second to none. Their variety and splendour will amaze. There are great thirty-foot-high paintings by Hogarth gracing the staircase and in the museum there is the cast of the explorer Livingstone's lion-bitten left humerus, along with the skull of John Bellingham who assassinated the prime minister Spencer Percival. Captain Shaw of the London Fire Brigade, he who was immortalized by Gilbert and Sullivan in *Iolanthe*, bequeathed his thrombosed aneurysm to St Bartholomew's and for more elevating contemplation the hospital's parish church of St Bartholomew the Less is richly representative of medieval as well as fifteenth- and eighteenth-century architecture.

The hospital's foundations were laid 'both in spirit and in stone' in 1123 by Rahere, who lies buried beneath a great canopied tomb in the church of St Bartholomew the Great. A sinful and worldly wit of a monk, he had led the creeping life of a courtier, indulging in 'carnal delights' while pouring

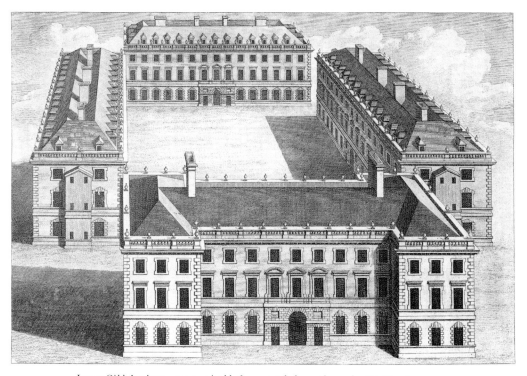

James Gibbs's plans – more suitable for a stately home than a hospital for the poor

pleasantries into princes' ears and arranging cushions under grandees' elbows or merely playing away his existence on a lute.

On a pilgrimage to Rome to purge his 'frivolities and triflings' he was struck down with malaria and 'reaching the limits of life' vowed to build a hospital for the poor if he recovered. St Bartholomew appeared to him in 'a vision full of awe and sweetness' saying that the hospital, as well as a church in his name, should be built at Smithfield in London. 'Under the shadow of my wings,' said the saint, 'I shall always defend and protect this place.'

He is there today, carved over the church porch, forever protecting the twelfth-century stones, but with wings seemingly too meagre to defend the hospital from the onslaught of the twentieth-century politician. Incidentally, St Bartholomew, one of the twelve apostles, who was flayed alive in martyrdom, has a butcher's knife as his emblem in art – a sorry symbol of today's slicing through of both meat market and hospital.

The church – where both Inigo Jones and William Hogarth were christened and where Benjamin Franklin worked as a printer in the Lady Chapel – was always described as 'beautiful as a picture' and so too is the hospital nearby.

You step into Barts beneath an ornate entrance arch, built in 1702 – and grand enough to grace a

Sir James Paget lecturing to medical students on the subject of feet and footwear

stately pile – by Edward Strong whose father, Sir Christopher Wren's chief mason, had carried the last stone to the top of St Paul's. A richly clad and carved Henry VIII stands proud beneath the pediment. He had refounded St Bartholomew's in 1546 after the dissolution of the monasteries had failed to close its doors, when the city successfully pleaded for help with all the 'myserable people lyeing in the streete,

offendyng every clene person passing by the way with theyre fylthie and nastye savors'.

One of St Bartholomew's most precious objects, its Royal Charter, granting the hospital to the City of London, was shakily signed by Henry VIII only a month before he died. In an archive collection matched by no other in the English-speaking world, there are over 2000 medieval deeds, as well as every

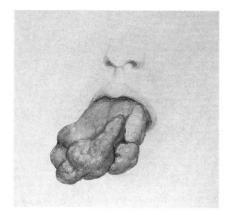

*(above) A delicate watercolour of a
diseased tongue*

*(right) Livingstone's left humerus, John
Bellingham's skull and Captain Shaw's
thrombosed aneurysm etc*

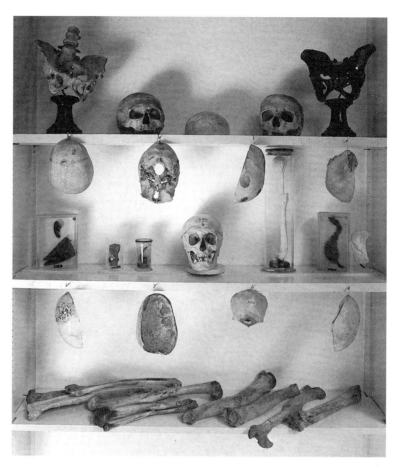

conceivable record of hospital life from the early
1500s including, for example, all the accounts since
1547 with their bills attached. This, I may say, gives
the merest flicker of an idea of what is to be found in
the strongrooms, deep in the sod of Smithfield. There
are innumerable medical records, such as the case of
James Chard, who was admitted with 'chimney
sweepers' cancer' in 1848, never having washed for
'five or six years at a time'. There is a wealth, too, of
watercolours, of most delicately painted indelicate

subjects. One, of a dreadful diseased tongue forever
trapped outside its unfortunate owner's mouth, is
accompanied with its case notes: 'The patient's sense
of dignity was so much offended at having to sit with
his tongue out, that he insisted on going out.'

Most ancient and symbolically stirring of all is the
hospital's original grant, written on a small piece of
parchment in 1137 and still hanging heavy with seals.
Cheek by jowl with such treasures is W.G. Grace's
cricket bat (he qualified at Barts) as well as James

Gibbs's original 1730s plans for his great buildings around the courtyard of the hospital. Described as 'the finest open air room in all England', this grand scheme still to a large extent survives. Disgracefully the South Wing was demolished in 1935 (although later rebuilt with many of the original stones). Despite this architectural hiccup, few more beautiful and soothing spots than this courtyard can be found in the heart of London.

The governors had always determined upon building a palace for the poor and the grand staircase alone is worthy of princes, with its two enormous works by Hogarth that cover the entire stairwell. In *The Pool of Bethesda* all the figures clustered around Christ were painted from patients at Barts in the 1770s. There is an alarmingly grey-faced sufferer of chlorosis and a baby with congenital syphilis. The other wall on which hangs *The Good Samaritan* was painted in situ, with Hogarth's pugnacious little person perched aloft on a scaffolding. Both he and Gibbs worked free for the hos-pital, little dreaming of the horrors in store from a vandalistic government 250 years hence.

Gibbs's monumental masterstroke is the Great Hall, a room that roars out the glory of St Bartholomew's and of all those who have nurtured its survival for eight-and-a-half centuries. Still clothed in its original sumptuous yet subtle tones, it is emblazoned with the names of the hospital's benefactors, all shining forth in gold from the walls. There are portraits, too, of all the teachers at St Bartholomew's – one of the first and greatest teaching hospitals in the world – set in ornate movable frames, to be wheeled at will around the room, thereby never interfering with the hall's decorative splendour. Barts is the proud possessor of works by Millais, Lawrence and Reynolds.

The sons and daughters of St Bartholomew's are legion. Timothy Bright, the inventor of shorthand, was physician in the 1580s and William Harvey, who discovered the circulation of blood, was physician between 1609 and 1645. Elizabeth Blackwell, the first woman doctor in the British Isles, studied in the hospital and Ethel Manson was a matron at Barts when she established the State Registration of Nurses in 1919 – she herself became SRN 1. Mozart had his tonsils out here in the 1770s and the poet Robert Bridges was the casualty physician in the 1870s.

How can such an institution as this be abandoned? It has been a general hospital serving London for almost a thousand years, building up unique and treasured traditions of service. These are irreplaceable, and if their continuity is broken, something of rare and inestimable value for present and future generations will be lost forever. There are schemes afoot for its salvation, the most beguiling being that it reopens as a charitable institution, free to the public and supported by private and city funds, thereby once again becoming 'a spiritual Sanctuary in stone' for the sick, the poor and 'the homeless wanderer' just as it was in 1123.

SRN 1

ZETA

'A closet or a chamber where
church documents were kept'

HE most beautiful parish library in Britain is to be found in the suburbs of Slough. Within the walls of St Mary the Virgin Church, hidden from view and only reached by walking through a covered pew, it was built by Sir John Kedermister in 1623.

After mile upon mile of harsh suburban sprawl, without any warning you are suddenly confronted with the rosy tones of an early seventeenth-century brick church, flanked on either side by tiny almshouses – each with a brick-pedimented doorway – dating from 1617. Originally a Norman church, St Mary's was enlivened by Sir John Kedermister, when he superintended the Royal estate of Langley nearby. Surprising as this oasis is, however, it gives no clue as to the startling rarity of the little chamber that awaits you inside. It is the chapel on the south side of the church that starts you wondering: on a raised floor, beneath which Sir John and his wife are buried, there is a long sweep of an ornate wooden screen – the outer wall of the Kedermisters' private pew. Almost carnival-like with its obelisks, flourishing strapwork and colours, it is painted to look like marble – off-white veined with grey – and with sunken panels of green and red speckled medallions. To shield the family from the rest of the congregation, delicately latticed

windows alternate with pierced Gothic and geometrical openings. The door swings lightly open, as do the windows – spindly fragile on their original hinges – and in you step to a world of absolute strangeness. It is a narrow passage of a pew, gazed upon from all sides by 'The Eye of God' – seventeen of them looking out from panels of grey clouds – painted with '*Deus Videt*'. Texts from the psalms are painted all around to remind you yet further that God sees. The original hat pegs are still sticking out from the walls and there are knobbed panels on the ceiling, to be slid aside for ventilation. One end the wall is emblazoned with the Kedermisters' heraldic achievements, while at the other – having walked through an arch painted with clouds overhead – to one's stupefied delight is the library.

Time after time, year in and year out, it will leave you breathless with surprise, as if clapped in a trap of its all-enveloping beauty. Framed grisaille cartouches cover the walls from floor to ceiling. The twelve apostles, as well as prophets, evangelists, doctors and fathers of the Church, are painted in brilliant colours, all in little individual wooden frames. Local and imagined landscapes and architectural views march round beneath the cornice – one is of Windsor Castle and another is thought to be of Langley Park, the great house that was given to Sir John Kedermister in 1626. There is also a little painting of the oak avenue that

'Clapped in a trap of all-enveloping beauty'

was planted from Langley to Windsor, of which only fragments remain today. A lone Eye of God looks down into the library.

With a pull of a tiny wooden knob, many of these walls open, revealing a *trompe-l'œil* of endearingly primitive open books. Some have dog-eared pages and others are painted with scarlet ribbons to tie them up. Another has a little marker sticking out of its pages. In one cupboard, Sir John Kedermister and his wife Dame Mary – bedecked in lace finery – pictorially preside over all. Beneath them, and all round the room, this mainly theological collection of books is handsomely and uniformly bound in the original brown calf, most of them blocked in gold with the Kedermister arms. Sir John founded his library 'for the benefit of Ministers of the said town of Langley and such other of the County of Buckinghamshire to resort thereunto'. One such, the Revd J. C. Wernedly, vicar of Langley in the 1660s, seemed to have reaped scholarly benefit – having by 1701 read the psalms in Hebrew thirty-three times and the whole of the Hebrew Bible no fewer than six times over. There are two volumes from the famed Plantin Press of Antwerp, one of which – produced in 1584 when Plantin himself was still alive – is the Bible in Greek,

Hebrew and Latin. The earliest work in the library is the French manuscript of Peter de Riga's *Aurora*, dating from the mid-1300s. The latest is the Speaker's Bible that was presented to Sir Edmund Seymour in the House of Commons in 1673. Their most precious possession – the eleventh-century illuminated manuscript *Gospels of the Winchester School* – is now on loan to the British Museum Department of Manuscripts. Although the original catalogue of 1638 shows that one or two of the original books are missing, some 250 remain.

Most improbable for the layman is Sir John and Dame Mary's 500-page 'Pharmacopolium' of 1630 with various and vile remedies: 'A special medecine to helpe the throate for one that cannot swallowe – for the Swelling of the Throat ... Take a white hard dogges turd, beate into a pouder, and take English honny and mingle them togeither, and spread it thicke upon a linnen clothe, and heate it against the fire and lay it all over the throate downe to the kennell bone, and change it with fresh morning and evening, and binde it hard thereto, and it helpeth. Probat.' (Tried and tested by Dame Mary!) The title page has all the finesse of an illuminated manuscript. 'The lord hath created medicines of the earth and hee that is wise will not abhorre them' is surrounded by a riot of wild strawberries and honeysuckle, pansies and butterflies. Some of the remedies held true to this uplifting maxim: 'A Medicine for the Swimming in the Head ... Take ii ounces of the buddes of Red roses and i ounce of good oyle of Roses, one ounce of Cowslipp-oyle and ii spoonfulls of a woman's milke of a male childs, and iii nutmegges finely beaten and seared and as much mace made into powder ... and a little red rose water and as much wine vinegar, and mingle all these together and warm it in a Chaffing-dish and annoynt y/e Crowne of the head and under y/e Eares, rubbe it very well in and keepe them hott

while it is doing and after ... probat'. For a gallstone, she recommended 'the seeds of blew and March violettes with a hare strangled with cord' and for 'the Biting of a Mad Dogge ... Take liver, lights and heart of the dogge and boyle them very dry, and let the partie eat some of it, and beate some of to powder and lett him drincke of it, untill three changes of the moone be past'. For 'those who cannot hold water' she recommended 'boiled claws of a goat'. She even claimed 'to knowe whether one that is Weake or Sicke shall Live or Die: Take the juice of the herb called mousehair and give the sicke to drinke and if he caste it up hee shall dye.'

The fireplace in the library is curiously at odds with the rest of the room. An obviously different and more delicate hand has produced an array of grotesquely indelicate creatures with ghoulish and pendulously bosomed satyrs parading along the mantelpiece. The overmantel bulges forth in a convex oval, painted gold and with the arms and alliances of the Kedermisters linked by chains. The four cardinal virtues – Providence, Justice, Temperance and Fortitude – are voluptuously represented on the supporting spandrels.

There is one tiny fly in the ointment – a carefully prepared and painted family tree in which Sir John was eager to show off his connection to Queen Elizabeth. It appears that after his great-great-grandmother had died, his great-great-grandfather married again to the great-great-great-grandmother of the Queen!

Every book in the library was restored in 1938–9, and slow restoration was carried out on the library between the 1930s and 1970. In 1981 vandals managed to force their way in, wrenching panels from the entrance arch. These have now been restored. At no other time since 1623, however, has this precious little room been touched.

SELECT BIBLIOGRAPHY

Aleph, *London Scenes & London People: Anecdotes, reminiscences etc.*, London 1863

Alexander, Eleanor, *Primate Alexander, Archbishop of Armagh: A Memoir*, London 1913

Anderson, Verily, *The Last of the Eccentrics: A Life of Rosslyn Bruce*, London 1972

Ashton, John, *Social Life in the Reign of Queen Anne, Vols I & II*, London 1882

Bardon, Jonathan, *Belfast: An Illustrated History*, Belfast 1982

Baring-Gould, S., *Early Reminiscences 1834 64*, London 1923

   Further Reminiscences 1864 94, London 1925

   Cornish Characters and Strange Events, London 1925

   The Vicar of Morwenstow, London 1886

Barnard, Julian, *Victorian Ceramic Tiles*, London 1972

Barrow, Andrew, *The Flesh is Weak*, London 1980

Bate, G. E., *And So Make a City Here*, Hounslow 1948

Bateman, Michael & Stenning, Shirley, *The Wit of the Church*, London 1967

Beckett, J. C., Belfast: *The Making of the City 1800 1914*, Belfast 1988

Bell, Walter George, *Fleet Street in Seven Centuries*, London 1912

Berkshire Archaelogical Journal, Volume 53, 1952 3

Bindman, David, *Hogarth*, London 1981

Bingham, Caroline, *The History of Royal Holloway College 1886 1986*, London 1987

Bolton, A.T., *The Portrait of Sir John Soane*, London 1927

Bowes, Q. David, *Encyclopedia of Automatic Musical Instruments*, New York 1972

Bradby, Christopher & Ridler, Anne, *Best Stories of Church & Clergy*, London 1966

Brennan, Flora, *Translations of Puckler's Progress*, London 1987

Brett, C. E. B., *Buildings of Belfast 1700 1914*, Belfast, 1967

Burrows, Margaret F., *Robert Stephen Hawker: A Study of his Thought and Poetry*, Oxford 1926

Buzas, Stefan, *Sir John Soane's Museum*, Berlin 1994

Cassidy, Raymond, *Copped Hall: A Short History*, Waltham Abbey 1983

Chapman, Pauline & Leslie, Anita, *Madame Tussaud: Waxworker Extraordinary*, London 1928

Child-Pemberton, W.S., *The Life of Frederick Hervey*, London 1925

Colloms, Brenda, *Charles Kingsley: The Lion of Eversley*, London 1975

Colvin, Howard, *Architecture and the After Life*, New Haven and London, 1991

   A Biographical Dictionary of English Architects 1660 1840, London 1954

Cone, John Frederick, *Adelina Patti, Queen of Hearts*, Hampshire 1994

Connor, Patrick, *Oriental Architecture in the West*, London 1979

   The Inspiration of Egypt (exhibition catalogue), Brighton 1983

Crompton, Alastair, *The Man who Drew Tomorrow*, Bournemouth 1985

Crook, J. Mordaunt, *William Burges and the Victorian Dream*, London 1981

Curl, James Stevens, *Eygptomania*, Manchester 1994

   A Celebration of Death, London 1980

Curtis, Bill, *Blackpool Tower*, Suffolk 1988

Dainton, Courtney, *The Story of England's Hospital*, London 1961

Dale, Tim, *Harrods: The Store and the Legend*, London 1981

Davies, E.W. L., *A Memoir of Jack Russell and his out of door life*, London 1878

Demoriane, Hermine, *The Tightrope Walker*, London 1989

Disraeli, Benjamin, Sybil: *The Two Nations*, London 1845

Dorment, Richard, *Alfred Gilbert*, New Haven and London 1985

Eltick, R. R., *Shows of London*, London 1978

Elton, Arthur, *The House that Jack Built: The Story of Marshall & Co.*, Leeds 1993

Esdaile, Mrs Arundel, *Temple Church Monuments*, London 1933

Eyre, Kathleen, *Seven Golden Miles*, Lancaster 1989

Fleury, Maurice, *Memoirs of Empress Eugenie*, New York and London 1920

Forsyth, Alastair, *Buildings for the Age: New Building Types 1900 39*, HMSO 1982

Girouard, Mark, *The Victorian Country House*, Oxford 1971

Goldin, Grace & Thompson, John D., *The Hospital: A Social and Architectural History*, New Haven 1975

Greenwood, Douglas, *Who's Buried Where in England?*, London 1982

Greenwood, Martin, *The Designs of William de Morgan*, Wiltshire 1989

Grott, Richard G., *Egyptian Revival: Its Sources, Monuments & Meaning 1808 58*, Berkeley 1978

Harvey, Anthony & Mortimer, Richard, *The Funeral Effigies of Westminster Abbey*, Woodbridge 1994

Head, Raymond, *The Indian Style*, London 1986

Headley, Gwyn & Meulenkamp, Wim, *Follies*, London 1986

Hinde, Thomas, *A Field Guide to the English Country Parson*, London 1893

Holland, Lady, *Sydney Smith*, London 1878

Huchon, Rene, *George Crabbe & His Times 1754 1832*, London 1907

Jones, Barbara, *Follies and Grottoes*, London 1953

Kebbell, T. E., *Life of George Crabbe*, London 1888

Kennedy, A. E. C., *Stephen Hales DD FRs: An Eighteenth Century Biography*, Cambridge 1929

Kilvert, Revd Francis, *Kilvert's Diary 1870 9*, London 1986

Kingsley, Charles, *The Lion of Eversley*, London 1975
The Water Babies: A Fairytale for a land baby, London 1885

Kositpipat, Chalermchai & Vijinthanasarn, Panya, *The Mural Paintings of Wat Buddhapadipa*, London 1970

Lane, Jane, *Titus Oates*, London 1949

Larmour, Paul, *Belfast*, Belfast 1987

Lasdun, Susan, *Victorians at Home*, London 1981

Mackenzie, W., ed., *Complete Works of William Hogarth*, London c. 1890

Maxwell, Gordon S., *Highwayman's Heath*, Hounslow 1935

Mayhew, Henry, *Morning Chronicle Survey of Labour and the Poor, Vol. I*, New York 1968

Medvei, V. C. & Thornton, J.L. eds, *Royal Hospital of St Barts 1123 1973*, distributed by the librarian, St Bartholomew's Hospital 1974

Millenson, S., *Sir John Soane's Museum*, Michigan 1987

Milne, J. Lees, *Worcestershire*, London 1964

Moorman, F.W., *Robert Herrick: A Biographical and Critical Study*, London 1841

Paulson, Ronald, *Hogarth*, London 1976

Pearson, Hesketh, *The Smith of Smiths, being the Life, Wit and Humour of Sydney Smith*, London 1945

Pevsner, Nikolas, *The Buildings of England* (various), Harmondsworth 1974

Physick, John & Darby, Michael, *Marble Halls*, London 1973

Portland, K. G., GCVO, Duke of, *Men, Women and Things*, London 1987

Pugh, Peter, *The Royal Bath*, Cambridge 1988

Purcell, William, *'Onward Christian Soldier': A Life of Sabine Baring-Gould 1834 1924*, London 1957

Reilly, D. R., *Portrait Waxes*, London 1953

Rheims, Maurice, *The Age of Art Nouveau*, London 1966

Rimmer, W. G. ed., *Marshalls of Leeds, Flaxspinners*, Cambridge 1960

Risley, Mary, *The House of Healing*, London 1962

Rose, Millicent, *The East End of London*, London 1951

Russell, Frank ed., *Art Nouveau Architecture*, London 1979

Russell-Cotes, Sir Merton, *Home and Abroad: Autobiography of an Octogenarian*, Bournemouth 1921

Sharp, Dennis, *The Picture Palace*, London 1969

South, Raymond, *The Story of Virginia Water*, Buckingham 1983

Stanley, Chris C., *Highlights in the History of Concrete*, British Cement Association 1979

Timpson, John, *Timpson's England*, Norwich 1987

Turner, Brian & Palmer, Steve, *The Blackpool Story* (booklet for Blackpool Festival), June 1994

Von Puckler Muskau, Prince M. L. H., *Tour in Germany, Holland and England in the Years 1826, 1827 and 1828, Vol. IV*, London 1832

Walker, J. W., *Wakefield: Its History and its People, Vol. II*, Wakefield 1939

Watkin, David, *The English Vision*, London 1982

Webster, Mary, *Hogarth*, London 1979

Wood, the Revd J. G., *My Backyard Zoo*, London 1887
Petland Revisited, London 1890
Petland, London 1890
Man & Beast, London 1874

Index

Places in Central London are entered under London. Places in Greater London are entered under their own names.

Arbroath mausoleum, 94–5
Ashton Hall, 107

Bedfont, 43, 44
Belfast
  Botanic Gardens, 8–9
  Cave Hill, 9
  Crown Liquor Saloon, 9–10
  Crumlin Road Gaol, 7
  Harland and Wolff shipyard, 10–11
  Linen Hall Library, 9
  McCausland's warehouse, 7
  Poor House, 6
  Presbyterian churches, 6, 11–12
  Queen's University, 7
  St Malachy's Roman Catholic Church, 6
  Scottish Providential Society, 9
  Titanic memorial, 11
  White Linen Hall, 6
  'Bendhu', Northern Ireland, 15–16
Blackpool
  Casino, 37
  'Golden Mile', 37
  Mogul circus, 36–7
  North Pier, 34
  Pleasure Beach, 37
  Tower, 34, 36
  Tower Ballroom, 32–3
  Winter Gardens, 33
Bournemouth
  East Cliff Hall, 18–22
Bray, Berks
  fishing temple, 117
Bridgend
  prisoner-of-war camp, 99
Bristol
  Art Nouveau, 3–4

Cambridge
  Old Addenbrooke's Hospital, 16
Cardiff Castle, 50
Castel Coch, 50
Chaldon
  Church of St Peter and St Paul, 80
Claydon House, Bucks
  Chinese room, 31
Cobham, Kent
  mausoleaum, 90
Cobham, Surrey
  Silvermere Haven, 77–8, 80
Compton, Surrey
  Art Nouveau, 4–5
Copped Hall, Essex, 83
Craig-y-Nos, 104, 106
Cranford, 43, 47
  St Dunstan's Church, 47–8

Davenport
  library and temple, 30
Down Hall, Essex, 14
Downhill, Co. Derry
  Mussenden temple, 72–3

Egham
  Holloway College, 77
  Holloway Sanitorium, 77

Farnborough, Hants
  St Michael's Abbey, 74, 75
Flintham Hall, 86–9
Fulham
  Craven Cottage, 26, 27–8

Gateshead
  cement works, 13
Gatton Park
  Doric temple, 120
Gravesend, 81
Great Warley
  St Mary's Church, 1, 82–3
Halstead, Essex
  The Railway Children, 80–1

Hamilton
  Hamilton Palace, 93
  mausoleum, 93–4
Harlington, Greater London, 43, 44
  church, 44
Harmondsworth, 43, 47
Henllan
  Italian chapel, 99–101
Hounslow, 46
Hounslow Heath, 43–4, 48

Isle of Bute
  Mount Stuart, 49–52
Isle of Sheppey, 13
  Ship on Shore, 14
Iver, 82

Jordans
  Quaker Meeting House, 82

Kensal Green
  cemetery, 61–3, 65, 68, 70
Kings Langley, 82
Kirtlington, 117

Lambholm, Orkney
  chapel, 96–7
Langley, Bucks
  parish library, 149–51
  St Mary the Virgin Church, 149
Leatherhead, 82
Lechlade
  Old Father Thames, 13
Leeds
  Egyptian temple, 30
  Gledhow Hall, 40
  Oriental Baths, 25
Leeds Castle
  grotto, 126
Leicester
  Royal Panoptican, 24–5
Limpsfield, 82
Little Stanmore
  mausoleum, 90, 92
Liverpool
  Art Nouveau, 1
London
  8 Addison Road, 40

Art Nouveau, 1, 2, 3
  Egyptian Hall, Piccadilly, 29
  Egyptian mausoleum, 31
  Great Eastern Hotel, 117–18
  Grosvenor Hotel, 14
  Houses of Parliament, 39
  Inverness Court Hotel, 102
  Kew glasshouse, 8
  Lincoln's Inn Fields, 53, 54
  Postman's Park, 40, 42
  Royal Courts of Justice Restaurant, 42
  St Bartholomew the Great Church, 144, 145
  St Bartholomew's Hospital, 144–8
  St Margaret's, Westminster, 82
  Sir John Soane's Museum, 53–4, 56, 58–60
  Smithfield, 145, 147
  University College, 138, 139
  Victoria and Albert Museum, 38
  waxworks, 134, 135, 136–8, 139
  Westminster Abbey, 136–8

Morwenstow
  vicarage, 131

Osborne House, 14, 39
Oxford
  St John's College, 17

Paris, 1, 74
Penzance
  Egyptian House, 29
Peterborough, 97–8
Plas Newydd, 102
Portland Hall, 13

Reading
  Abbey, 13

Rhum
  Kinloch Castle, 108, 110–12
Rome, 13

St Albans, 82
Sale
  Ritz cinema, 25
Salisbury
  Cathedral spire, 13
Stanford Hall, 102–4
Stanwell, 43, 44
Stoke Poges, 82
Stoke Row
  Maharajah's Well, 23–4
Stokesay Castle, 140–43
Stow Bardolph, 138
Stowe, Bucks
  Chinese House, 31
Sway
  concrete tower, 14

Temple Bar, 84–5

Virginia Water, 118–20

Waddesden
  underground caves, 126
Waltham Abbey, 82
Ware
  Scott's grotto, 122–3
Welbeck Abbey, 123–5
Wemyss Bay Railway Station, 49
West Horsley, 82
Wimbledon
  Southside House, 113–16
  Thai Buddhapidipa Temple, 121
Windsor
  Art Nouveau, 1–2
  Home Farm dairy, 39–40
Woking
  Brookwood Cemetery mausolea, 95
  Shah Jehan Mosque, 23, 24
Wootton, Beds
  picture palace, 107